MW00475374

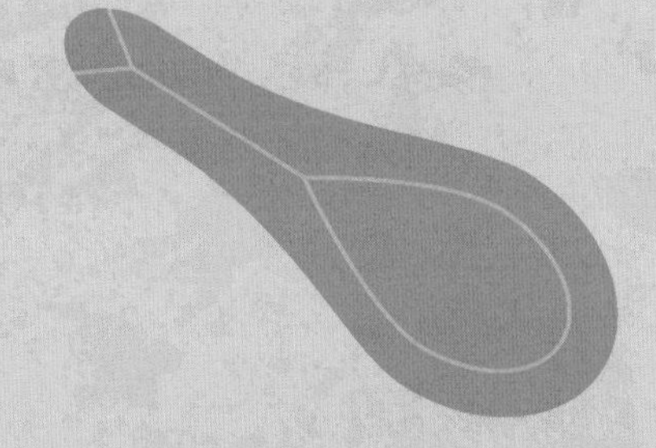

BOWLFUL

Norman Musa

BOWL FULL

Fresh and vibrant dishes from Southeast Asia

PAVILION

Contents

Introduction

It is always a joy to cook Southeast Asian dishes that are packed with diverse ingredients, rich in herbs and spices and have such exquisite flavours. For someone like me who grew up in that part of the world, and is now living abroad cooking these dishes for friends and family, it brings back memories of my childhood, and of the exciting travels I embarked on to discover authentic regional dishes.

The region that comprises Malaysia – where I grew up – Thailand, Indonesia, Singapore, Myanmar, Vietnam, Laos, Cambodia and the Philippines, is rich with wonderful dishes and having been there to see the culture and culinary diversity for myself, it has always been my dream to share these experiences in the recipes I created for this book.

During my travels, I discovered a great number of similarities in the way that people across Southeast Asia enjoy serving their food in bowls. Ceramic bowls are a must for every household – from small ones for noodles and rice, to medium and large bowls in which to serve dishes for everyone to share. For cafés and street food stalls, melamine-type bowls are the most common, as they do not damage easily and are economical too.

Bowlful includes 80 main recipes using methods that are accessible and easy to follow; there is a good selection of plant-based dishes, together with seafood, poultry and meat dishes. The recipes I have created are based on the daily home-cooked food of the region, plenty of street food dishes and some I have adapted using local Western produce, plant-based products and beans.

In addition to suggesting alternative ingredients for any that cannot be easily sourced, I also share many tips for cooking with Asian ingredients. The recipes are created for individual small bowls for two and four servings, and also for medium to large bowls for four or more servings.

Bowlful is ideal for beginner home cooks who want to learn more about Southeast Asian cuisine and gradually build up their confidence using Asian ingredients – with all the dishes beautifully presented in bowls.

Southeast Asian Cuisine & Eating Culture

This region that encompasses people of multi-ethnic backgrounds and traditions with a vast range of cuisines makes it one of the most visited areas in the world for its food and culture.

Due to their geographical closeness, the cuisines of Malaysia, Thailand, Myanmar, Singapore and Indonesia share many common spices and herbs. The food of Vietnam is rather different, with many dishes focusing on fresh herbs, grilled meat or fish and soup dishes, compared to countries like Thailand, Malaysia and Indonesia, where dishes are heavier, with a large number of herbs and spices included in each dish, as well as the extensive use of coconut milk in curries. Myanmar is different again, with distinctive curries cooked without coconut milk, while the Philippines is known more for its stews.

There are some dishes with certain similarities that have sparked debates on their precise origin, but this happens even when a dish has come from outside the region – for example, Hainanese chicken rice, which was claimed by both Malaysia and Singapore, even though it was well-known that the dish actually came from Southern China. These discussions reflect this history of both migration to the region, and also colonization by foreign powers. For example, the Vietnamese dish, *banh mi* (see page 122) as derived from French influence, and dishes in the Philippines from Spanish cuisine.

Some parts of Southeast Asia were also on the historic Silk Road, with Malacca in Malaysia being a trading post for merchants to exchange commodities, and this greatly influenced the local cuisines, especially in Malaysia, which is regarded as the ultimate melting pot and embodies the very essence of diversity within the region.

Rice is a staple food in the region and is consumed every day as well as being eaten in different forms, such as noodles, rice paper and many more. A typical rice dish is eaten with others made of meat, seafood or vegetables.

Daily meals in the region start with breakfast, when rice and noodles are consumed as an option; then there is a light snack mid-morning; rice with a curry or stir-fry for lunch; a light afternoon snack, mostly comprising fried dishes; dinner is something grilled or fried at a food court or stretch of food stalls; and the day finishes with a late supper at the eateries that are mostly open 24 hours.

The warm and humid weather influences the eating culture greatly, with all the outdoor stalls and cafés for people to meet up with friends or spend time with family eating out. It is a common thing to see small children still awake past midnight eating with their families – an eating culture or habit that you will not see in any Western countries.

The eateries that are open until the early hours cater for the foodies and the buzz from these noisy stalls and food hawkers, especially at the weekends, creates a wonderful atmosphere.

The Bowlful Cupboard

Choosing the right products to keep in your kitchen cupboard can be a bit tricky as there are so many products used in Southeast Asian cooking that you could possibly end up with a large number of ingredients that you only use once or twice.

The recipes I have included in this book are mainly intended as weekday meals, with the idea that they are something simple that uses easily sourced ingredients. I hope this encourages you to cook dishes from the book two or three times a week and if you do that, you will use up the items in your cupboard more quickly.

When it comes to size, I always prefer to buy small bottles or jars of things like soy sauce or sesame oil, so I know they will get used up before the expiry dates. The same goes for any products that have a shelf life of 12 months or less – it is wise to buy a small quantity so they are not wasted by not being used within the time period.

It is advisable to check product labels on how to store them correctly once they have been opened as some are best kept in the fridge.

Listed on the next few pages are all the essential products that I recommend you keep in your kitchen cupboard.

CHILLI SAMBAL

Buying a ready-made chilli paste or sambal in a jar makes cooking easier, but choosing the right one for the dish is important to create a good balance of spiciness without being overpowering. Making your own sambal is good but there are some really good ready-made sambals available in the supermarkets. I recommend sambal oelek or badjak for my recipes, not just for their level of spice but also for the colour. The dark, rich red colour is the one to go for. The best chilli sambals are made from dried chillies, tamarind, sugar, onion and garlic.

SWEET CHILLI SAUCE

This is a great condiment or dip made from chilli, rice vinegar, garlic, ginger and sugar. I make sure I have a bottle of this in my kitchen cupboard at all times. The brands Mae Ploy and Pantai are the best quality and I use these a lot as a dip or salad seasoning.

FISH SAUCE

Fish sauce is used a lot in Thai and Vietnamese cuisines and is another great source of seasoning. It is made from salted anchovies and krill, a type of crustacean, and is a good alternative to shrimp paste. Not everyone is a fan of shrimp paste but it does add a good flavour to dishes. 1 teaspoon of shrimp paste can be replaced with 1 tablespoon of fish sauce.

MUSHROOM STIR-FRY SAUCE

This is my alternative flavouring to oyster sauce that I use in my vegan dishes. The shiitake mushrooms used to make the sauce add rich, umami and earthy flavours.

NOODLES

There are many different types of noodles to choose from. My favourite three that I always keep in my cupboard are vermicelli, flat rice (5mm/¼in or 1cm/½in wide) and fine or medium egg noodles. Most Asian supermarkets stock 400g (14oz) packets and you can easily find smaller packets of 200g (7oz) in local supermarkets; 200g (7oz) is enough for four people either for a stir-fry or for a soup or broth. Boiled noodles can be kept in the fridge for up to four days. I don't recommend freezing noodles as the texture is not as nice as freshly boiled noodles.

OYSTER SAUCE

This sauce is sweet and salty and provides dishes with umami and caramel flavours. It is made from oyster extract and sugar, and the saltiness comes from the oysters. It can be used to replace dark soy sauce.

PALM SUGAR

This is a sugar produced from the sap of palm trees and is widely used in Southeast Asian cooking. It comes in block form or in a tub. For my cooking, I slice the blocks thinly and measure the sugar into tablespoons, so that it dissolves easily in the dishes. An alternative is coconut sugar, but if sourcing either of these is difficult where you live, you can use soft light brown sugar.

RICE

There are two types of rice I usually keep in my kitchen cupboard, in small quantities – basmati and jasmine. Basmati is used for rice recipes that are cooked with stock, meat or vegetables, as the grains stay separate and are not soft and sticky like jasmine rice. For white rice to serve with curries or stir-fries, I prefer jasmine rice as it is slightly stodgy and absorbs sauce or gravy better. For fried rice, leftover basmati or long grain rice is the best, but it works with jasmine rice too if you refrigerate it for an hour or overnight and separate with your fingers or put in a ziplock bag to break up the grains ready for frying. Rinsing the raw rice until the water runs clear makes it less starchy once cooked. This is why there is a tradition for Southeast Asian households to wash the rice at least three times. This also used to be for reasons of hygiene as in the paddy fields, before the rice husks were picked, they would be dried in the sun in the open air.

RICE VINEGAR

This is my go-to source of acidity for all my salad seasonings and dipping sauces. It is made from fermented rice, and is the complete opposite to distilled white vinegar as rice vinegar is sweet and delicate, not sharp and acidic like distilled white vinegar. Alternatively, you can use apple cider vinegar, lime juice or lemon juice. For dressings, I combine lime juice and rice vinegar to give a good, strong, sweet and acidic flavour to the dish. If you don't have rice vinegar, you can replace it with white wine vinegar and add a bit of sugar to give it the sweetness of rice vinegar.

SESAME OIL

This toasted oil with a rich, earthy and nutty flavour is used in my recipes for flavouring and is added towards the end of cooking.

SHIITAKE MUSHROOMS

Of all the types of mushrooms available, these are my favourite to add to dishes for their earthy, umami and buttery taste. I often keep a packet of dried shiitake mushrooms in my cupboard and they only need to be soaked in boiling water for 10–15 minutes, depending on their size. For anything larger than 5cm (2in) in diameter, you may need to soak them for up to 30 minutes to hydrate fully. You can tell when the mushrooms are ready by squeezing them: when the texture has become spongy and they release water, they are ready for cooking.

SHRIMP PASTE

Known as *belacan* (Malaysia), *terasi* (Indonesia) and *kapi* (Thai), this is used as a seasoning in a similar way to fish sauce. To enhance the flavour, the paste is usually toasted to release the aroma. Doing this in a frying pan creates a strong smell that lingers in your kitchen. Alternatively, you can wrap the paste in aluminium foil and fry it like that; not everyone is keen on the smell and toasting is not compulsory, but it will make your dish taste better. You can also buy paste that has already been toasted from Asian supermarkets, as well as in powder form. Wrap any leftover paste in paper and keep in an airtight container.

DARK SOY SAUCE

This is used in my recipes for its sweet and salty flavour, and also for the colour. The sauce is made from molasses (black treacle), wheat, soya beans and salt. It is salty but the molasses gives it a good balance of salty and sweet, unlike light soy sauce which is added to dishes for seasoning. There are many different brands of dark soy sauce, so always look out for the slightly thicker type with a rich dark colour. It is not necessary to keep the bottle in the fridge once it has been opened, as it can be kept in the cupboard like other types of soy sauce, but keeping it in the fridge does make the flavour last longer.

LIGHT SOY SAUCE

The type of light soy sauce I use in this book is widely available in all supermarkets and adds flavour without colouring the rice or noodles – in other words making the dish darker. It is made of fermented soya beans and wheat. Chinese light soy sauce is my favourite and I usually use it with sweet soy sauce to create a good balance of sweet and salty flavours in a dish. It is also the best type to use for dressings and dips, which I usually combine with sesame oil. Light soy or mushroom sauce is a great vegetarian alternative for fish sauce.

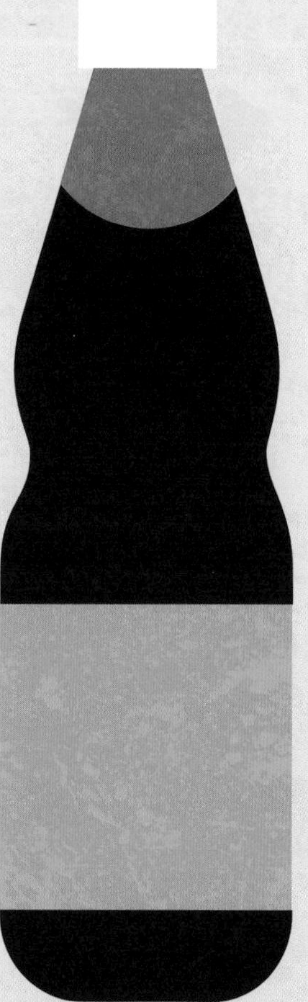

SWEET SOY SAUCE

Also known in Indonesia as *kecap manis,* I highly recommend having this in your cupboard as this is one of the key ingredients for rice and noodle dishes. Adding it to curries gives a wonderful caramelized flavour. It is made from fermented soya beans, together with palm sugar and spices, which gives it a rich, caramel, sweet and slightly salty flavour. Some sweet soy sauce is quite thick and too sweet for my taste; I would choose one that is slightly runny. My favourite is always the Malaysian Habhal's sweet soy sauce. Combining both light soy sauce and *kecap manis* in rice and noodle dishes creates a good balance of sweet and salty flavours. See the recipe intro on p68 (Beef in Spicy Soy Sauce) for how to make your own sweet soy sauce.

TAMARIND

This is a souring agent that complements any spicy dish. Adding tamarind reduces the heat of the chilli. You can buy three types of tamarind in Asian supermarkets – pulp, concentrate and paste. You can sometimes find tamarind pods, but these are eaten as a snack as they are a sweet tamarind and not used in cooking. I use paste in all my recipes; if your paste is very thick and highly concentrated, use slightly less. Tamarind pulp, which is less expensive, contains stones. To make it into a paste, add 200ml (7fl oz/scant 1 cup) of hot water to 4 tablespoons of pulp, leave to soak for an hour and then pass through a sieve to extract the stones. If you are using tamarind concentrate, which is less flavoured, use 2 tablespoons for every 1 tablespoon of the quantity of paste listed in my recipes.

Spices

If you are a keen cook, having a good range of spices in the cupboard is essential for Southeast Asian cooking. Below is a list of spices you should have in your cupboard, either in ground form or as seeds.

BLACK PEPPERCORNS

Peppercorns kept in a grinder is my favourite way to store them. Freshly ground pepper has a wonderful pungent, warm and woody flavour.

CARDAMOM

This is a strong spice that is commonly used for rice dishes. There are two types of cardamom: the pale green that give a spicy, rich aroma with a hint of lemon and mint; and black cardamom pods that is smoky with a strong smell. I use green cardamom in all my recipes and usually I don't crush them before I add them to a dish so that the aroma does not become too overpowering.

CINNAMON

There is a difference between cinnamon bark and cinnamon sticks. The former is made from the outer bark of the tree and is used for medicinal purposes. Cinnamon sticks are made from layers of the inner bark that are rolled together; the flavour is sweeter and more delicate. I use cinnamon sticks measuring 5cm (2in) in my recipes.

CLOVES

This is one of my favourite spices to add to my cooking. Its sweet smell makes rice dishes in particular wonderfully fragrant. It is a great antioxidant, and in Malaysian cooking, cloves belong to the 'four friends' spice group, along with cinnamon, star anise and cardamom. These are added to soups, stews and curries.

CORIANDER

Small and round with a hint of a lemony citrus aroma, coriander seeds are one of the key ingredients for spice paste in Southeast Asian cooking. For my recipes, I use ground coriander to keep things simple, but if you would rather make it from scratch, toast the seeds over a low heat for 1 minute and then grind them until you have a fine, smooth powder. Keep in an airtight jar and store in a cool, dry place to maintain freshness.

CUMIN

Earthy with a strong nutty flavour, cumin has a distinctive aroma that works well with meat. I prefer to use cumin seeds, crushing themusing a pestle and mortar.

CURRY POWDER

Ground mixed spices also known as curry powder, is a mixture of basic ground spices ranging from chilli, turmeric, coriander, cumin and fennel, combined with the likes of cinnamon, star anise, fenugreek, mustard, nutmeg, cloves or any other spices, depending on what it is being cooked with, whether it is meat, seafood or vegetables. To make your own basic ground mixed spices, you can mix 1½ tablespoons of ground coriander, and 1 teaspoon each of ground turmeric, chilli, cumin and fennel. Apart from making your own, buying a ready-made curry powder from a supermarket, such as Madras curry powder, is also suitable for my recipes.

FENNEL

These seeds are harvested from the plant's flowers and then dried. They have a sweet aniseed and liquorice flavour, and are particularly good in fish and seafood dishes. This is one of the spices that I always have in my cupboard.

FENUGREEK

The seeds, also known as *methi*, have a distinct tangy, bitter taste, and are usually added to rice.

FIVE-SPICE

A mixture of ground star anise, cinnamon, fennel, Szechuan pepper and cloves, this blend of spices has a sweet, liquorice and pepper flavour. You can make your own by mixing 2 teaspoons each of ground black pepper, fennel and star anise with 1 teaspoon each of ground cinnamon and cloves.

MUSTARD SEEDS

In my cooking, I use black mustard seeds as the flavour is stronger and you only need a small amount; for pickles and light flavourings, I use yellow or brown mustard seeds as they are milder. The seeds are great for fish or seafood curries.

NUTMEG

This warm and nutty spice is available as a seed or in ground form. I recommend you use the seeds that, when grated, release a distinct sweet aroma; you only need to add a little.

PAPRIKA

Ground paprika is a mixture of dried ground peppers and chillies. It is not commonly used in Southeast Asian cooking and it is added to some of my recipes to achieve a rich, red colour without the heat of chilli powder. However, if you prefer spicy dishes, feel free to replace all the ground paprika in my recipes with chilli powder, but be careful of the heat (I recommend mild to medium chilli powder). Avoid using smoked paprika as the flavour is too strong for these dishes.

STAR ANISE

This spice is used a lot in Southeast Asian cooking in curries and soups for its sweet, liquorice and pepper aroma. Star anise comes in pods that you can break into individual petals. You don't have to add whole pods to your dishes, you can add individual petals in groups of eight to your dish instead, or you can crush or grind them to make ground star anise.

TURMERIC

One of the most used spices in Southeast Asian cooking, turmeric comes as a fresh root, a paste and in ground form. In recent years, fresh turmeric has become readily available in local Asian supermarkets and online. Every 5cm (2in) of fresh turmeric can be replaced with 1 teaspoon of ground turmeric. As turmeric root usually comes in packets of 100g (3½oz) and only a little is used at a time, you can freeze what is left over, but make sure you peel the roots before freezing they can become soft when defrosting.

One common question I am asked in my masterclasses is how to remove turmeric stains. If your fingers are stained, rub them with lime or lemon juice, which helps the colour fade more quickly. For kitchen equipment or knives, wipe with rice vinegar and let it work overnight.

Other Asian Ingredients

COCONUT MILK

Two of my favourite brands of coconut milk are Chaokoh (Thailand) and Kara (Indonesia). For any other brands, check the percentage of coconut milk and anything that contains more than 70 per cent coconut extract is good to use. As I always remind my masterclass students, freeze any leftover coconut milk in an ice cube tray – each cube is the equivalent of 1 tablespoon of coconut milk.

JACKFRUIT

For anyone who has never cooked with young green jackfruit before, don't be alarmed by its bland taste – it is cooked for its texture. Ripe jackfruit has sweet, yellow flesh and is eaten raw. Jackfruit curry was one of my late mum's favourite dishes to cook for the family. She bought fresh jackfruit from the market and once she had cut it into small pieces, she boiled the pieces until tender and then added them to the curry. In recent years, cooking with jackfruit has become so trendy it is now readily available in supermarkets. For canned jackfruit that comes in brine or water, give it a good rinse before cooking.

TEMPEH

I could easily give up a meat dish for a tempeh dish if you put them next to one another. Tempeh is made from fermented soya beans and is high in protein and fibre. It is loved for its texture and nutritional benefits rather than its taste. The dense texture makes it suitable for stir-fries and curries, but I could just as easily eat it as a snack after I have fried the pieces lightly until golden brown and seasoned them with salt, pepper and ground paprika. There are many independent and artisan tempeh producers these days, and a favourite of mine with a nice firm texture is produced by London-based ProTempeh. Tempeh is suitable for home freezing; I recommend cutting it into 1cm (½in) thick slices, and putting them in a ziplock bag or container before freezing.

TOFU

There are different types of tofu with various textures; for my recipes, I recommend firm tofu. Also known as bean curd, tofu is made from soaked and crushed soya beans, which are then boiled with salt and acid to separate the bean curd and whey. Frying firm diced tofu lightly in oil helps to firm up the outside and stops the tofu from breaking up. As the taste is quite bland, you can always season it with salt before adding to dishes. If you have any tofu left over, I recommend dicing it into 3cm (1¼ in) cubes and frying it lightly in a little oil. Once it has cooled, you can season with salt and then freeze it. Frozen diced tofu can be added straight into dishes without having to defrost it first; it takes about 3–5 minutes cooking time for the cubes to defrost fully. Tofu puffs are another type of tofu with a spongy texture that I use in my recipes. The puffs are light and hollow in the middle and are good in soups and curries.

BAY LEAVES

Bay leaves can be used as an alternative to curry leaves, and for any of my recipes that use bay leaves, you can also use curry leaves instead. If you are using fresh bay leaves, remove them once the dish is cooked as the strong, bitter flavour can become slightly overpowering if they are left in the dish for too long. If you are using dried leaves, you can leave them in the dish as the flavour is more subtle.

CHILLIES

Most of my recipes use the fresh red or green chillies with the seeds removed, but if you like your dishes on the spicy side, leave in the seeds. If you want even more heat, add two or more small bird's eye chillies. I always keep a jar of dried chillies handy in my kitchen in case I run out of fresh chillies. Dried chillies have to be soaked in hot water until they are soft before you can use them like normal chillies. I recommend Kashmiri dried chillies. Any leftover chillies can be blended with a dash of rice vinegar, kept in a jar and refrigerated for future use. The vinegar makes the chilli paste last longer.

FRESH CORIANDER

Coriander stalks and leaves are used in many of my recipes as a garnish or made into curry pastes. Coriander root is used in Thai curries to give a pungent, peppery flavour, but sourcing it can be tricky as it is only available in some Asian supermarkets. As an alternative, I add coriander stalks and ground cumin to give that pungent flavour. To keep coriander fresh, rinse the leaves in cold water, blot dry with kitchen paper, put them in a ziplock bag and then store them in the fridge as they last longer at cool temperatures.

CURRY LEAVES

Fresh curry leaves give dishes a tangy, sharp aroma and can be found in Indian grocery shops. I am not as keen on dried curry leaves as the aroma is almost non-existent; unlike other herbs the aroma of curry leaves does not last. If sourcing curry leaves is difficult where you live, you can replace them with bay leaves – which is what I always do. For leftover curry leaves, the best option is to put them in a jar with vegetable or coconut oil, so the oil is infused with the flavour and can then be used as cooking oil.

GALANGAL

In the same family as ginger, galangal has a distinctive citrusy, peppery flavour. Adding too much can make your dish taste slightly overpowering. You can replace galangal by adding extra ginger, together with 1 teaspoon of lime juice. It also comes in a dried form that needs to be soaked in lukewarm water for at least 20–30 minutes before it is ready to use. The galangal root that is available in Asian supermarkets has a smooth, light brown skin that needs no peeling, unlike ginger.

GINGER

Fresh ginger root is an essential ingredient in Southeast Asian cooking. It is available fresh in root form, ground (as a dry powder) or as paste in a jar. Using the fresh root is the best way to get that strong, pungent, sharp, peppery flavour. I use a teaspoon to peel the skin off the ginger root to avoid wasting too much of the flesh.

KAFFIR LIME LEAVES

It is unusual to find fresh kaffir lime leaves in Asian supermarkets as they are generally sold frozen, and frozen ones are better than the dried leaves. Unlike curry leaves, frozen kaffir lime leaves retain their flavour and fragrance. Tearing the leaf ribs enhances their zesty aroma, and in all my recipes, I slice the leaves thinly so that they can be eaten as part of the dish rather than being left on the side.

LEMONGRASS

Lemongrass is a fragrant, fibrous herb that gives dishes a fresh, zesty flavour. Only use the white part of the stalk as it is tender and easier to blend when turning it into a paste. Lemongrass can be kept frozen, and slicing it into small pieces beforehand makes it easier to blend straight from the freezer.

MINT

Fresh mint is commonly used as a garnish in Southeast Asian cooking. In Vietnamese cuisine in particular, mint, fresh coriander and Thai basil are always served with noodles, salads and pancakes. To keep the leaves fresh, wrap them in damp kitchen paper and store them in the fridge.

SPRING ONIONS

I often use spring onion as a garnish. My favourite is to cut the green part of the onion – which has a stronger taste – into thin strips and soak in cold water to make beautiful curls. The white part can be thinly sliced and fried in oil in a similar way to shallots or garlic, something that I always do for fried rice or stir-fries.

THAI BASIL

Thai basil has a sweet flavour with a hint of aniseed. Widely used in Thai and Vietnamese cuisine, it adds a distinctive flavour and can also be used as a garnish – I prepare my leaves by frying them in vegetable oil until crispy. If sourcing Thai basil is difficult, use Italian basil as an alternative and sprinkle with a pinch of ground star anise to replicate the flavour.

A GUIDE TO BOWLFUL

When it comes to serving food in bowls, it is not just the presentation that matters, it is also about the function of the bowl and how it is used. Without making things too complicated and thinking more about creating a feel-good mood around serving delicious food in bowls, I have classified a few different bowls, which is really more about the style than the type of bowl itself, to act as a guide to serving the dishes my way. This is not just to complement my recipes, but perhaps to encourage you to consider including them in your kitchen cupboard – just a thought. It is not essential, but after all, food is all about having fun serving up your dishes in fun and creative ways, just like I present them in this book.

Solo Bowls

I have included many great and simple recipes for two, and a solo bowl is one that is big enough for one serving, like a pasta bowl, for example, but my favourite is deep enough for a bowl of noodle soup. Returning from a busy restaurant kitchen, my kind of comfort food is something simple in my favourite bowl: the bowl that I take to the UK and the Netherlands, or to wherever I go to work for a longer period. These solo bowls work well for recipes like salads, noodles or rice. For any of my recipes for two or four servings, or if you are cooking just for yourself, it is always nice to save leftovers for the next day.

Communal Bowls

Eric, a Dutch friend of mine, showed me the best way to serve dishes like stir-fries is together with rice in a large bowl for us to share. This is unusual in Asia as usually we prefer to put rice in our individual bowls. Served in a large, single bowl, this avoids any leftover rice, which I think is a smart way to cut down on food waste from individual plates or bowls. For this kind of bowl, a serving will be enough for two or more people to share.

Signature Bowls

Don't you like to show off a little when you have cooked such delicious food? Well, this is how you should do it. My sister Melissa, in the Netherlands, loves her Royal Albert Old Country Roses bowls and plates and only takes them out of her glass display cabinet for special occasions. I have a few in my collection and do the same: you will see various recipes using my signature bowls that are close to my heart.

Tapas Bowls

These are small bowls like cereal bowls and the little bowls that are served in Chinese restaurants. There are many great recipes that would be suitable for dinner parties, served in nicely decorated bowls. Forget about the washing up that you will need to do when all the bowls have been used, but instead think about the wonderful presentation that will certainly impress your guests.

Sal

Meat & Seafood

Vegetarian & Plant-based

Plaice & Salad Bowl

I chose plaice for this ceviche-style cured fish and salad bowl as it has a distinct umami-like taste that blends perfectly with Asian herbs. This dish originates from Sarawak, Malaysia and is one of many great delicacies from the region. It is important to choose a very fresh fish for this recipe. Other raw fish that can be used are halibut, mackerel, flounder and sole. You can use smoked salmon instead of plaice if you are not keen on raw fish.

SERVES 4

2 large, very fresh skinless plaice fillets, about 150g/5½oz each, cut into bite-sized chunks
2 tbsp rice vinegar
1 banana shallot, thinly sliced
5 garlic cloves, finely chopped
2.5cm/1in ginger, finely chopped
2 red chillies, deseeded and cut into thin strips
juice of 2 limes
1 cucumber, spiralized into noodle-like strips
1 unripe mango, peeled, stoned and cut into thin strips
1 red onion, sliced into thin rings
175g/6oz rocket salad
salt and pepper

In a large bowl, mix the plaice chunks with the vinegar and leave for 5 minutes. Squeeze out the excess vinegar from the fish and transfer to a clean bowl, together with the shallot, garlic, ginger, chillies and lime juice. Mix well and refrigerate for 30 minutes.

In a separate bowl, add the cucumber, mango and red onion, and mix well to combine. Season with salt and pepper to taste. Divide the rocket salad between four serving bowls and then add the cucumber salad and fish mixture on top. Serve at once.

Maureen's Burmese Lethoke

Maureen Duke is a wonderful friend of mine who was born in Burma (now Myanmar). She has taught me a great deal about Burmese cuisine and has generously allowed some of her best recipes to be included in this book. Lethoke was the first dish she introduced me to, and my version is a simple lethoke salad with egg noodles, vegetables and dried shrimps.

For the vegan version, replace the dried shrimps with finely chopped crispy fried tofu, and the fish sauce with light soy sauce.

SERVES 2

100g/3½oz fine egg noodles
100ml/3½fl oz/scant ½ cup coconut oil (or olive oil)
1 medium onion, halved and thinly sliced
1 medium carrot, shredded or julienned
1 courgette, shredded or julienned
3 tbsp dried shrimps, soaked in warm water for 10 minutes, drained and finely chopped
juice of ½ lemon
1 tsp fish sauce
1 tbsp tamarind paste

Cook the noodles according to the instructions on the packet; drain and set aside.

Heat the oil in a saucepan over a medium heat and fry half of the onion until golden brown. Remove with a slotted spoon and transfer to a plate. Keep the oil to use for seasoning the salad.

In a bowl, mix the egg noodles, carrot, courgette, half the fried onion (keep the rest to garnish the salad), the remaining raw onion, 2 tablespoons of the oil, the shrimps, lemon juice, fish sauce and tamarind. Mix well and if you need more flavour, adjust by adding more fish sauce, lemon juice and oil.

Transfer to two serving bowls and keep refrigerated for 15 minutes, then garnish with the remaining fried onion before serving.

Crunchy Green Salad

This vegan salad is made using all green vegetables and fruit with the added crunch of pistachios and pumpkin seeds.

For the dressing, I combined honey, soy sauce and ginger to provide the Asian flavour.

SERVES 2

1 Little Gem lettuce, cut into 3cm/1¼in pieces
½ cucumber, thinly sliced
2 celery sticks, cut into 2cm/¾in pieces
1 avocado, halved, stoned, peeled and cut into thin strips
1 courgette, julienned

FOR THE DRESSING

1 tbsp light soy sauce
2 tbsp virgin olive oil
2 tsp sesame oil
½ tbsp rice vinegar
juice of ½ lemon
1 tbsp honey
2 tsp grated ginger

FOR THE GARNISH

1 red chilli, deseeded and cut into thin strips
1 tbsp pistachios, lightly crushed
1 tbsp pumpkin seeds

Put together all the ingredients for the dressing in a large bowl and mix well.

Toss the lettuce, cucumber, celery, avocado and courgette with the salad dressing and divide between two serving bowls. Garnish with the chilli, pistachios and pumpkin seeds. Serve immediately.

Soy & Ginger Chicken with Glass Noodle Salad

Glass noodles, also known as cellophane noodles, are made from mung beans which give them their transparent look, not like the vermicelli noodles that are made from rice. The noodles I use are from China; in Korea and Japan the noodles are made from sweet potato. You can cook the chicken on a barbeque, or oven bake in the oven at 180°C fan/200°C/gas mark 6 for 20–25 minutes or until cooked through. If sourcing glass noodles is tricky where you live, use vermicelli noodles.

SERVES 4

150g/5½oz glass noodles
4 boneless chicken thighs, about 125g/4½oz each
½ tbsp vegetable oil
1 red onion, halved and thinly sliced
10 cherry tomatoes, halved
10 sprigs of fresh coriander, leaves picked
10 fresh mint leaves
2 tbsp pomegranate seeds
100g/3½oz/scant 1 cup salted peanuts, coarsely crushed

FOR THE MARINADE

5cm/2in ginger, grated
2 tbsp sweet soy sauce
½ tsp coarsely crushed black pepper

FOR THE DRESSING

2 tbsp fish sauce
3 garlic cloves, finely chopped
1 tbsp palm sugar
juice of 1 lime
1 tbsp rice vinegar

Soak the noodles in lukewarm water for 15 minutes, drain and set aside.

Put the marinade ingredients in a large bowl, together with the chicken, and leave to marinate for 10 minutes.

To make the dressing, put all the ingredients for the dressing together in a bowl and mix well.

Heat the oil in a heavy-based frying pan or skillet over a medium-high heat. Cook the chicken for 5 minutes on each side until nicely browned and cooked through. Lift out and place in a bowl and allow to cool for 5 minutes, then place on a board and cut into slices 2cm/¾in thick.

In a large bowl, mix together the noodles, onion and tomatoes with the dressing. Transfer to four serving bowls, divide the chicken between them and garnish with the coriander, mint, pomegranate seeds and peanuts. Serve immediately.

Prawn Vermicelli Salad

This exotic salad includes fresh herbs and is perfect for a barbeque. I prepared this for my friends and marinated the prawns in sweet chilli sauce, cooked them on a hot barbeque for 2–3 minutes and then served them with the vermicelli, mango and tomato salad. I recommend using very thin vermicelli noodles for this salad as they absorb the dressing nicely. Check my recommendation for the best brand of sweet chilli sauce to use on page 12. My tip is to cook the prawns on a hot barbeque, but alternatively, you can cook them on a griddle pan as described below.

SERVES 4

150g/5½oz vermicelli noodles
8 extra-large raw king prawns, heads and shells on
2 tbsp shop-bought sweet chilli sauce
2 tomatoes, halved and deseeded, cut into thin strips
1 unripe mango, peeled, stoned and sliced into thin strips
1 cucumber, halved, deseeded and cut into thin strips

FOR THE DRESSING

2 tbsp fish sauce
3 garlic cloves, finely chopped
1 tbsp palm sugar
juice of 1 lime
1 tbsp rice vinegar

FOR THE GARNISH

10 fresh Thai basil leaves
10 sprigs of fresh coriander, leaves picked
100g/3½oz/scant 1 cup salted peanuts, lightly crushed
4 tbsp pomegranate seeds
1 lime, cut into 4 wedges, to serve

Cook the noodles according to the instructions on the packet, drain and set aside.

In a large bowl, toss the prawns with the sweet chilli sauce and leave to marinate for 10 minutes.

Put all the dressing ingredients into a large bowl, give them a good mix and add the noodles, tomatoes and mango. Toss everything well together and set aside to allow the noodles to absorb the dressing.

Heat a griddle pan over a high heat and cook the prawns in batches for 3–4 minutes until pink and opaque. Transfer to four serving bowls, together with the salad, and top with the garnish ingredients. Serve immediately with a squeeze of lime – one wedge for each bowl.

Jackfruit Salad

My late parents were very proud of the jackfruit tree in their front garden. When it was in season, the tree bore so many fruits that they gave them away to their friends and neighbours. In Southeast Asia, it is very common to grow jackfruit trees in gardens, as they require very little maintenance. Young jackfruit are harvested to be cooked in curries or as part of a salad, and the ripe fruit, when the flesh turns yellow and sweet, can be eaten as it is. For this salad, the jackfruit is combined with carrot and runner beans, and seasoned with lemongrass, chilli and coconut milk to give an exotic salad flavour.

SERVES 4

200g/7oz runner beans, cut diagonally into thin strips
1 medium carrot, cut into thin strips
2 x 565g/20oz cans jackfruit in brine, rinsed, drained and cut into thin slices
1½ tsp coarsely ground black pepper
juice of 1 lime, plus extra to finish
2 tbsp desiccated coconut, lightly toasted

FOR THE DRESSING

1 tbsp vegetable oil
1 banana shallot, thinly sliced
2 stalks of lemongrass, thinly sliced
2 red chillies, deseeded and thinly sliced
100ml/3½fl oz/scant ½ cup coconut milk
1½ tsp fine sea salt
½ tbsp palm sugar

Put the beans and carrot in a pan of boiling water and blanch for 1 minute; drain and set aside.

To make the dressing, heat the oil in a medium frying pan over a medium heat and fry the shallot, lemongrass and chillies for 1 minute, then add the coconut milk, salt and sugar and cook for 1 minute, then turn off the heat. Set aside and cool completely.

In a large bowl, toss the beans, carrot and jackfruit with the dressing until all the ingredients are well mixed. Add the pepper and lime juice and stir again. Transfer to a large serving bowl and sprinkle over the desiccated coconut, then add a final squeeze of lime juice if preferred. Serve immediately.

Gado Gado Salad

I was never very keen on using ready-made peanut butter to make peanut sauce as I usually prefer to make everything from scratch – including toasting the peanuts – in my attempt to prepare dishes authentically. However, this all changed after I tried the 'cheat' version, but I am still picky about which peanut butter I use. For this recipe, crunchy peanut butter is the best type to use. One thing is for sure, this easy method is a time saver. Using freshly grated lemongrass adds to the flavour. Exclude the eggs for a vegan option.

SERVES 4

1 tbsp vegetable oil
400g/14oz firm tofu, drained and cut into 1cm/½in-thick slices
400g/14oz cooked baby potatoes, halved, served warm
200g/7oz fine beans, trimmed at both ends and cut diagonally into 4cm/1½in pieces
1 medium carrot, sliced diagonally into pieces
100g/3½oz baby spinach
100g/3½oz bean sprouts
4 eggs, boiled for 8 minutes, cooled, peeled and halved
1 Little Gem lettuce, halved, stems removed and the leaves picked individually
4 baby cucumbers, cut in half lengthways

FOR THE PEANUT SAUCE

200g/7oz/xx cup crunchy peanut butter
½ tbsp chilli paste (I recommend sambal badjak)
1 stalk of lemongrass, white part only, grated
1 tbsp sweet soy sauce
½ tbsp tamarind paste
salt

Heat the oil in a medium frying pan over a medium-low heat and fry the tofu in batches for 2 minutes or so on each side until firm and crispy on the outside. Remove from the pan and set aside.

Bring 500ml/18fl oz/generous 2 cups of water to the boil and blanch the beans and carrot for 2 minutes. Remove with a slotted spoon, and using the same water, continue with the spinach and bean sprouts for 30 seconds. Remove, transfer to a plate and blot with kitchen paper.

For the peanut sauce, put all the ingredients into a medium bowl with 200ml/7fl oz/scant 1 cup of boiling water and mix well.

Put the sauce into four serving bowls and neatly place all the salad ingredients next to each other in the bowls. Serve immediately.

Poached Cod & Salad

Toasted rice powder is a key ingredient in Northern Thai and Lao cuisines and is used in salads or as the thickening agent in stews and curries. For my home-made version, I use sticky rice, slowly toasted in a dry frying pan over a low heat for about 10 minutes until light brown, then I put it in a spice grinder to turn it into powder form. For this salad, you can also use other types of white fish, such as haddock or halibut.

SERVES 4

200ml/7fl oz/scant 1 cup fish stock
500g/1lb 2oz skinless cod fillet, cut into 4 pieces

FOR THE DRESSING

2 tbsp fish sauce
3 garlic cloves, finely chopped
1 red chilli, deseeded and finely chopped
1 tbsp palm sugar
juice of 1 lime
1 tbsp rice vinegar

FOR THE SALAD

200g/7oz fine beans, cut diagonally into 4cm/1½in pieces
1 cucumber, cut in half lengthways, deseeded and cut diagonally into pieces 1cm/½in thick
1 banana shallot, thinly sliced
1 stalk of lemongrass, thinly sliced
100g/3½oz watercress
1 tbsp toasted rice powder, (see above)
10 fresh mint leaves, roughly chopped
10 sprigs of fresh coriander, leaves picked

Put all the ingredients for the dressing in a small bowl and mix well. Set aside.

Pour the fish stock into a pan, bring to the boil, then turn the heat down to low. Add the fish and poach for 2 minutes. Remove with a slotted spoon and put in a bowl, together with the salad dressing. Set aside to marinate for 10 minutes.

For the salad, put the beans in a bowl, pour over boiling water until well covered and leave for 1 minute. Drain, transfer to a large bowl, then add the cucumber, shallot, lemongrass, watercress and toasted rice powder. Toss everything well together and divide between four serving bowls.

Divide the fish between the bowls, pour over the dressing and garnish with mint and coriander leaves. Serve immediately.

Curries

& Stir-fries

Fish & Seafood

Cod & Fennel in Green Curry

When it comes to cooking a good curry, I prefer mine to be less creamy with not as much coconut milk, which can subdue the flavour of the herbs and spices. I recommend using a good-quality coconut milk by checking the percentage of coconut on the back of the can: you should look for one with more than 70 per cent pure coconut milk. In this curry, I love how the sweet, dense and flaky cod blends well with the strong flavour of the curry paste. This curry also works well with monkfish, halibut, scallops or lobster (cut into small pieces with the shells left on).

SERVES 4

2 tbsp vegetable oil
20 fresh Thai basil leaves
1 tbsp palm sugar
1 tsp fine sea salt
2 tbsp fish sauce
1 tbsp tamarind paste
1 fennel bulb, the top trimmed and cut into 8 pieces
600g/1lb 5oz skinless cod fillets, cut into 4cm/1½in pieces
200ml/7fl oz/scant 1 cup coconut milk
rice, to serve

FOR THE PASTE

1 banana shallot, peeled
3 garlic cloves, peeled
2 stalks of lemongrass, trimmed
5cm/2in galangal, or ginger with 2 tsp lemon juice
3 green chillies, deseeded
5 kaffir lime leaves, or zest of 1 lime
25g/1oz fresh coriander
1 tbsp ground coriander
1 tsp ground cumin
1 tsp ground white pepper

Blitz together the paste ingredients with 2 tablespoons of water using a handheld stick blender or food processor until fine and smooth.

Heat the oil in a deep saucepan over a low heat and fry the Thai basil leaves for 1 minute or until crispy. Take care as the leaves may pop and the oil spit when the leaves start to cook. Remove the leaves with a slotted spoon and set aside to use as a garnish.

Using the oil left in the saucepan, increase the heat to medium and stir in the paste, sugar, salt, fish sauce and tamarind. Cook for 3 minutes or until fragrant.

Stir in the fennel and cook for 2 minutes until the pieces have wilted.

Add the cod and coconut milk with 200ml/7fl oz/scant 1 cup of water. Bring to the boil and reduce the heat to low, then let it simmer for 3–5 minutes until the cod flakes easily.

Carefully divide the mixture between four serving bowls with some rice and garnish with the fried Thai basil. Serve immediately.

Padprik Prawn Stir-fry

'Pad' in the Thai language means fry and 'prik' means chilli. This is a popular Thai dish that is also known as a dry red curry and can be cooked with meat and seafood too. For my simple version, I use big, juicy prawns fried with fine beans, carrot and onion.

For the paste, you can use around 3 tablespoons of shop-bought Nam Prik Pao Thai chilli paste, but it is actually quite easy to make your own as you can see below. This can become a vegan dish if you replace the prawns with firm tofu and the fish sauce with soy sauce.

SERVES 2

2 tbsp vegetable oil
20 fresh basil leaves
1 red onion, cut in half and thinly sliced
100g/3½oz fine beans, both ends trimmed and cut into pieces 4cm/1½in long
1 medium carrot, cut in half lengthways and sliced diagonally
20 raw king prawns, shelled and deveined, but with tails on
1 tbsp sweet soy sauce

FOR THE PASTE

1 banana shallot, peeled
3 garlic cloves, peeled
2 red chillies, deseeded
1 tbsp rice vinegar
1 tbsp tamarind paste
½ tbsp palm sugar
1 tbsp fish sauce

Blitz together the paste ingredients with 2 tablespoons of water using a handheld blender or food processor until fine and smooth.

Heat the oil in a large wok or frying pan over a medium-low heat and fry half the Thai basil leaves for 1 minute or until crispy. Take care as the leaves may pop and the oil spit when the leaves start to cook. Remove the leaves with a slotted spoon and set aside to use as a garnish.

Using the oil left in the wok or pan, increase the heat to medium, stir in the onion and cook for 1 minute, then stir in the paste. Cook for 2 minutes then add the beans and carrot and continue to cook for 2 more minutes.

Add the prawns, together with 100ml/3½fl oz/scant ½ cup of water, and cook for 2 minutes until the prawns have turned pink. Add the soy sauce and give everything a good stir.

Turn off the heat, spoon into two serving bowls and garnish with the fried Thai basil leaves.

Squid Sambal

During the peak squid season between April and August, the fresh local Asian markets are full of squid laid out on the counters, some covered in ink burs, and some that contain roe. It is a typical habit of Asian shoppers to pinch the tubes to check and then select any squids that contain roe. The squid are easy to catch during the hours of darkness as they are attracted to lights – the fishermen flash lights from the boats to encourage the squid to come closer. I always find cooking squid can be tricky as it turns rubbery easily. My recommended cooking time below is for a tube 10cm/4in long, but bear in mind that once you have turned off the heat, the residual heat will continue to cook the squid; for smaller tubes, reduce the cooking time accordingly.

SERVES 4

1kg/2lb 4oz squid
2 tbsp vegetable oil
1 tbsp tamarind paste, or juice of ½ lime
1 tbsp palm sugar
2 tbsp fish sauce
1 tsp salt
2 onions, cut into thin rings
10 sprigs of fresh coriander roughly chopped, for the garnish
jasmine rice, to serve

FOR THE PASTE

1 banana shallot, peeled
3 garlic cloves, peeled
1 stalk of lemongrass, trimmed
4 red chillies, deseeded
100g/3½oz tomato purée

Clean and prepare the fresh squid. Pull the tentacles away from the body and cut off the bottom part that contains the ink. Remove and discard the quill from inside the tube.

Blitz together the paste ingredients with 2 tablespoons of water using a handheld stick blender or food processor until fine and smooth.

Heat the oil in a wok or large frying pan over a medium heat. Stir in the paste and cook for 3 minutes. Next, add the tamarind (or lime juice), sugar, fish sauce and salt, cook for 2 minutes and then stir in the squid and onions. Continue to cook for 3 more minutes and then turn off the heat.

Spoon into four serving bowls, serve with jasmine rice and garnish with the coriander.

Salmon & Aubergine Stew

This is my favourite dish for winter, or for when you are in the tropics, the rain is heavy and the breeze is cool, and you are craving a bowl of soup with a hint of chilli heat. The typical Malaysian style is for the paste to be made just with chillies; that is a bit too spicy for me but not for chilli lovers. My version is made using a Romano red pepper and tomatoes, blended with chilli to give a mild taste but that still maintains a red colour. I prefer this dish served with bread rolls but you can always opt for rice, preferably jasmine, or vermicelli noodles.

SERVES 4

1 large aubergine
2 tbsp vegetable oil
10 sprigs of fresh coriander, roughly chopped, plus extra for the garnish
10 fresh mint leaves, plus extra for the garnish
2 tbsp tamarind paste, or juice of 1 lime
1 tbsp fish sauce
1 tsp salt
½ tbsp palm sugar
600g/1lb/5oz salmon fillet, skinned and cut into 4cm/1½in pieces
200ml/7fl oz/scant 1 cup fish stock
salt and pepper
4 white or multigrain bread rolls, to serve

FOR THE PASTE

1 Romano red pepper, deseeded
3 ripe tomatoes, deseeded
4 red chillies, deseeded
2 stalks of lemongrass, trimmed
1 banana shallot, peeled
3 garlic cloves, peeled
5cm/2in fresh turmeric, peeled, or 1 tsp ground turmeric

On a chopping board, cut the aubergine into round slices 1cm/½in thick, brush with 1 tablespoon of the oil and season with salt and pepper.

Blitz together the paste ingredients using a handheld stick blender or food processor until fine and smooth.

Heat a griddle or frying pan over a medium-high heat and cook the aubergine for 2 minutes on each side until nicely charred and cooked through. Cook in batches if the pan is not big enough.

Heat the remaining oil in a large saucepan over a medium-high heat and stir-fry the coriander and mint for 30 seconds, then stir in the paste and continue to cook for a further 3 minutes, stirring every minute.

Next, add the tamarind (or lime juice), fish sauce, salt and sugar, and cook for 2 minutes. Gently add the salmon pieces and cook for 1 more minute to coat and seal the fish and then stir in the stock. Bring to the boil, turn down the heat to low and simmer for 5 minutes or until the dish is cooked and the fish flakes easily.

Turn off the heat, spoon into four serving bowls and garnish with extra coriander and mint leaves. Serve with bread rolls, or rice or noodles if preferred.

Prawn & Asparagus Stir-fry

If you are using fresh lemongrass, which is still firm and brittle, I highly recommend you grate the white part to release the strong fragrant, but if you are using frozen lemongrass, blitzing it with a handheld stick blender or chopping it finely is recommended.

This quick stir-fry dish is using coconut water, the type that you can use from the can or box that can be easily sourced from the supermarket. Leftover coconut water can be frozen in ice cube trays for future cooking. Remember, 1 ice cube is equivalent to 1 tablespoon (15ml). You can try this dish with lychee juice too, for something different.

SERVES 2

12 large raw king prawns, shelled and deveined, but with tails on
1 stalk of lemongrass, grated or finely chopped
1 tbsp fish sauce
½ tbsp palm sugar
1 tbsp vegetable oil
1 banana shallot, finely chopped
3 garlic cloves, finely chopped
1 red chilli, deseeded and cut into thin strips
10 medium asparagus spears, each cut into 3
½ tsp fine sea salt
100ml/3½fl oz/scant ½ cup coconut water
6 sprigs of fresh coriander, leaves picked
rice, for the garnish, to serve

In a large bowl, marinate the prawns, lemongrass, fish sauce and palm sugar together for 5 minutes.

Heat the oil in a wok or large frying pan over a high heat and stir-fry the shallot, garlic and chilli for 2 minutes, then add the prawns with the marinade and cook for 2 minutes until the prawns turn pink. Remove from the pan, place in a serving bowl and set aside.

Add the asparagus and salt to the wok or pan and cook for 1 minute, stir in the coconut water and cook for 2 minutes. Return the prawns to the wok or pan, mix well and turn off the heat.

Divide the stir-fry between two serving bowls with some rice and garnish with the coriander.

Mussel, Artichoke & Pineapple Stir-fry

Here the lemongrass, chilli and fresh herbs make this dish an exotic explosion with a citrusy flavour, a hint of chilli heat and sweet and sour from the pineapple. Traditionally, this dish would contain banana flower/blossom; artichoke hearts have a similar texture and this is my way of making this dish more straightforward by using an alternative that is easier to source.

SERVES 4

1 tbsp vegetable oil
1 banana shallot, finely chopped
3 garlic cloves, finely chopped
2 stalks of lemongrass, white part only, thinly sliced
1kg/2lb 4oz mussels, debearded and cleaned
250g/9oz pineapple, peeled, cored and cut into bite-sized chunks
2 x 280g/10oz jars artichoke hearts in brine, drained
vermicelli noodles or rice, to serve

FOR THE SEASONING

2 tbsp fish sauce
1 tbsp rice vinegar
1 tsp ground turmeric
2 tsp mild chilli powder

FOR THE GARNISH

1 red chilli, deseeded and thinly sliced
2 tbsp roughly chopped fresh chives
2 tbsp roughly chopped fresh parsley

Mix the seasoning ingredients together well with 2 tablespoons of water in a small bowl.

Heat the oil in a large wok or frying pan and stir in the shallot, garlic and lemongrass. Cook for 2 minutes, then add the mussels and seasoning mixture, give everything a good stir and then cover the pan. Continue to cook for 3 minutes, stirring every minute.

Uncover the pan, stir in the pineapple and artichokes and cook for 2 more minutes. Turn off the heat and discard any unopened mussels.

Transfer the stir-fry to four serving bowls with some vermicelli noodles or rice, and garnish with the chilli, chives and parsley. Serve immediately.

Pan-fried Mackerel & Curry Sauce

I love the strong flavour of mackerel. For this recipe, I fried the mackerel fillets separately to crisp up the skin, flavoured with tamarind, and put them on top of the curry sauce.

SERVES 2

2 mackerel fillets (skin on), about 300g/10½oz in total, cut into strips 5cm/2in wide
1 tbsp tamarind paste
½ tsp salt, plus 1 tsp extra
1 tbsp vegetable oil
2 banana shallots, thinly sliced
2 tbsp shop-bought mild curry powder
½ tsp sugar
4 sprigs of fresh coriander, leaves picked
1 lime, cut into wedges
50ml/1¾fl oz/3 tbsp coconut milk
rice, to serve

Rub the mackerel all over with the tamarind and ½ teaspoon of salt.

Heat the oil in a large, non-stick frying pan over a medium heat.

Fry one of the shallots for 3 minutes or until golden brown. Remove with a slotted spoon and dab with kitchen paper. Set aside to use as a garnish later.

Using the same pan, fry the fish strips skin-side down for 2–3 minutes on each side. Remove and put next to the fried shallot.

Still using the same pan and over a medium heat, sauté the second shallot until golden brown. Add the curry powder, sugar and the extra teaspoon of salt, together with 200ml/7fl oz/scant 1 cup of water and cook for 2 minutes.

Pour the sauce into a serving bowl and put the mackerel on top. Pour over the coconut milk and garnish with fried shallots, coriander and lime wedges. Serve with rice.

Grilled Sea Bass

The dressing for this dish is actually served as a dipping sauce, and works well if you are using the whole fish, which is how it is traditionally cooked. My simple version uses sea bass fillets with the dressing poured over and is served with rice. If you have a pestle and mortar, pound the dressing ingredients together as they do in Asian kitchens, but watch out in case it spits and splashes. The trick is to pound the dry ingredients first – the garlic, lemongrass, chilli, coriander and sugar – and then stir in the tamarind and fish sauce.

SERVES 2

1 tbsp vegetable oil
2 sea bass fillets (skin on), score the skin about 2cm/¾in apart
rice, to serve

FOR THE DRESSING

5 garlic cloves, finely chopped
1 stalk of lemongrass, thinly sliced
1 red chilli, deseeded and finely chopped
10 sprigs of fresh coriander, finely chopped
1 tbsp palm sugar
2 tbsp tamarind paste
2 tbsp fish sauce

Mix all the dressing ingredients together well with 2 tablespoons of water in a small bowl and set aside.

Heat the oil in a large frying pan over a medium-high heat and fry the sea bass skin-side down for 4–6 minutes, until the skin has turned crispy. Flip over and finish on the other side for 1 minute or so until the fish is cooked through.

Transfer the fish into two serving bowls with some rice and spoon over the dressing. Serve immediately.

Caramelized Prawn & Courgette Stir-fry

For a stir-fry, I always prefer to cook using peeled prawns so that the marinade can penetrate the flesh. For curries or stews, I go for prawns with the shells and heads on for that extra flavour. This dish is very quick and simple to prepare; the important thing is to get the sweet, caramelized sauce thickened up nicely, and it has to be served as soon as it is ready, straight from the wok or frying pan. The sauce gets very thick if you let it sit for too long in the pan before serving, but it will not be completely ruined. It can be reheated with a splash of water to thin the sauce again.

SERVES 2

12 large raw king prawns, shelled and deveined, but with tails on
1 tbsp vegetable oil
1 courgette, about 300g/10½oz, sliced into rounds 1cm/½in thick
1 banana shallot, finely chopped
3 garlic cloves, finely chopped
1 lime, ½ for the juice and the other half cut into 2 wedges for the garnish
egg noodles or rice, to serve

FOR THE MARINADE

1 tbsp fish sauce
2 tbsp sweet soy sauce
2 tbsp soft light brown sugar
1 tsp coarsely ground black pepper

FOR THE GARNISH

1 spring onion, cut into thin strips and soaked in cold water until curled, then drained
½ red chilli, deseeded and thinly sliced

In a large bowl, mix the marinade ingredients together well with the prawns and set aside for 5 minutes.

Heat the oil in a large wok or frying pan over a medium-high heat and fry the courgette for 2 minutes on each side. Cook in batches if the pan is not big enough. Remove with a slotted spoon and place the rounds on a plate lined with kitchen paper, then blot away any excess oil.

Using the remaining oil in the wok or pan, still over a medium-high heat, fry the shallot and garlic for 2 minutes and then stir in the prawns with the marinade. Cook for 2–3 minutes until the prawns have turned pink but are not yet fully cooked; stir in the courgette rounds and cook for a further minute or until the prawns are cooked.

Turn off the heat and squeeze over the juice of ½ lime. Give the pan another good stir and then spoon out into two serving bowls with some egg noodles or rice. Garnish with the spring onion, chilli and lime wedges. Serve at once.

Grilled Sea Bass p. 50

Caramelized Prawn & Courgette Stir-fry p. 51

Oven Baked Fish Curry

This is my favourite Cambodian fish curry dish. The traditional way to cook this dish, known as Trey Amok, is by steaming in small baskets made of fresh banana leaves. For my baked version, I put the fish curry in ramekins, but you can use any ovenproof bowls. The egg in the mixture binds the ingredients and makes the curry set nicely.

MAKES 4 RAMEKINS

100g/3½oz baby spinach
2 tbsp vegetable oil
1 tbsp palm sugar
2 tbsp fish sauce
1 tbsp tamarind paste
200ml/7fl oz/scant 1 cup coconut milk, plus extra for the garnish
500g/1lb 2oz skinless white fish fillets, such as cod, haddock or monkfish, cut into bite-sized chunks
2 eggs, lightly beaten
1 red chilli, deseeded and julienned
4 kaffir lime leaves, ribs removed and thinly sliced
rice, to serve

FOR THE PASTE

2 banana shallots, peeled
5 garlic cloves, peeled
2 stalks of lemongrass, trimmed
5cm/2in fresh turmeric, peeled, or 1 tsp ground turmeric
3 red chillies, deseeded
5cm/2in galangal, or ginger with 2 tsp lemon juice

Preheat the oven to 160°C fan/180°C/gas mark 4.

Blitz together the paste ingredients with 2 tablespoons of water using a handheld stick blender or food processor until fine and smooth.

In a medium bowl, blanch the spinach in boiling water for 30 seconds. Remove and pat dry with kitchen paper. Set aside.

Heat the oil in a wok or deep saucepan over a medium heat and fry the paste for 3 minutes until fragrant.

Stir in the sugar, fish sauce and tamarind, cook for 2 minutes and then stir in the coconut milk, together with 200ml/7fl oz/scant 1 cup of water. Bring to the boil, reduce the heat and simmer for 2 minutes, then turn off the heat.

Divide the fish and spinach between four medium ramekins or ovenproof bowls. Pour an equal amount of curry sauce into each bowl, stir well but gently, and make sure the spinach is visible in each ramekin or bowl.

Next, divide the beaten eggs between the bowls and mix gently. Put the bowls into a large, deep oven tray and pour in cold water so it reaches halfway up the bowls. Cover the tray with aluminium foil and seal around the edges to trap the steam.

Bake for 20 minutes, remove the foil and bake for a further 20 minutes.

Remove from the oven and set aside for 2 minutes, then pour ½ tablespoon of extra coconut milk over each bowl and garnish with the chilli and kaffir lime leaves. Serve with rice.

Prawn & Thai Basil Stir-fry

This great street food dish can be cooked in minutes. It is a dish that comes with white rice that you would order at a night food stall on busy Asian streets. Adding Thai basil makes it very fragrant, but if sourcing it is difficult where you live, replace with Italian basil and add a couple of pinches of ground star anise to give the aniseed flavour that Thai basil would bring.

SERVES 2

12 large raw king prawns, shelled and deveined, but tails left on
½ tbsp fish sauce, plus ½ tbsp extra for cooking
2 tbsp oyster sauce
2 tsp palm sugar
1 tbsp vegetable oil
3 garlic cloves, finely chopped
1 red chilli, deseeded and finely chopped
10 fresh Thai basil leaves, plus extra for the garnish
1 medium white onion, halved and thinly sliced
2 tomatoes, each cut into 8 pieces
rice, to serve

In a small bowl, season the prawns with ½ tablespoon of the fish sauce and set aside for 5 minutes.

In a separate bowl, add another ½ tablespoon of fish sauce with the oyster sauce and sugar, together with 100ml/3½fl oz/scant ½ cup of water. Mix well.

Heat the oil in a wok or large frying pan over a medium-high heat and fry the garlic and chilli for 30 seconds, then add the Thai basil and cook for a further 30 seconds.

Next, add the prawns and fry for 1 minute or until the prawns have turned pink but are not yet fully cooked.

Stir in the sauce mixture, together with the onion and tomatoes. Cook for 2 minutes until the prawns are cooked through and the vegetables are wilted.

Spoon into two separate serving bowls with a serving of rice and garnish with extra Thai basil leaves. Serve immediately.

Salmon Fish Curry & Greens

Rice is usually eaten at lunchtime and in Malaysia a typical set rice lunch would be a selection of meat, fish or seafood, with vegetables and also a condiment like achar, sambal or salted egg, served with white rice. This way of serving rice with mixed dishes is known as *nasi campur*. Here this salmon fish curry is accompanied by poached pak choi and rice.

SERVES 4

2 tbsp vegetable oil
1 tsp fine sea salt
½ tbsp palm sugar
2 tbsp fish sauce
600g/1lb 5oz skinless salmon fillet, skinned and cut into 4cm/1½in pieces
150g/5½oz fine beans, both ends trimmed and cut into pieces 4cm/1½in long
2 tbsp frozen peas
200ml/7fl oz/scant 1 cup coconut milk
a handful of fresh coriander, for the garnish
1 lime, cut into 4 wedges, for the garnish
jasmine rice, to serve

FOR THE PASTE

1 banana shallot, peeled
3 garlic cloves, peeled
2.5cm/1in ginger
3 green chillies, deseeded
2 stalks of lemongrass, trimmed
5cm/2in fresh turmeric, peeled, or 1tsp ground turmeric

FOR THE GREENS

4 pak choi, quartered
1 tbsp oyster sauce
2 tsp sesame oil

Blitz together the paste ingredients with 2 tablespoons of water using a handheld stick blender or food processor until fine and smooth.

Heat the oil in a large, deep saucepan over a medium heat. Fry the paste for 2 minutes.

Next, add the salt, sugar and fish sauce and cook for 1 minute. Add the salmon, beans and peas, gently stir to coat and cook for 2 minutes, then stir in the coconut milk and 200ml/7fl oz/scant 1 cup of water.

Bring to the boil and simmer over a low heat for 3 minutes until the fish is cooked through and the beans have wilted. Stir gently once or twice. Turn off the heat.

For the greens, put the pak choi in a medium, deep saucepan with 2 tablespoons of water. Cover the pan and cook over a medium heat for 5 minutes with the steam trapped inside. Open the lid and stir well. Turn off the heat and discard any juices. Next, pour in the oyster sauce and sesame oil, and mix well.

Spoon the salmon curry and pak choi into four serving bowls with some jasmine rice. Garnish with the coriander and lime wedges, and serve at once.

Steamed Sea Bass with Asian Dressing

The sauce in this dish is one of my most used dressings and can also be used to dress a salad. The fragrant herbs help to lift the flavour of any dish but it should always be prepared just before it is needed.

You can cook this dish using a whole sea bass as they do in the Far East, but allow an additional 10 minutes for steaming.

SERVES 2

300g/10½oz pak choi, cut into strips 3cm/1¼in wide
8 cherry tomatoes
2 sea bass fillets (skin on) approx 150g/5½oz per fillet
½ tsp fine sea salt
½ tsp ground white pepper
2 spring onions, cut into thin strips and soaked in cold water until curled, then drained
½ red chilli, deseeded, julienned and soaked in cold water for 10 minutes or more
jasmine rice, to serve

FOR THE DRESSING

3 garlic cloves, crushed
1 tsp grated ginger
1 stalk of lemongrass, thinly sliced
½ red chilli, deseeded and finely chopped
1 tbsp chopped fresh coriander, plus extra for the garnish
1 tbsp fish sauce
2 tbsp light soy sauce
½ tsp palm sugar
juice of ½ lime

Set a steamer ready.

Mix all the dressing ingredients together well in a small bowl and set aside.

Place a heatproof bowl in the steamer, put the pak choi and cherry tomatoes into the bowl, cover and steam for 5 minutes.

Season the sea bass with the salt and white pepper. Put the sea bass on a board and roll up the fillets from the tail end with the skin on the inside, exposing the sea bass flesh on the outside. Put the sea bass on the pak choi in the steamer, cover and steam for 10 minutes.

Lift the lid and pour the dressing over the sea bass; replace the lid and steam for a further 5 minutes.

Turn off the heat, carefully remove the bowl from the steamer and garnish with the spring onions, chilli and extra coriander. Serve with jasmine rice.

Curries

Meat & Poultry

Javanese Lamb Curry

I adapted this dish from the famous Javanese dish known as Tongseng. I chose a pointed cabbage as it is sweeter and milder than other types and goes well with lamb. I added more than is used in the traditional dish to give good balance of protein and vegetables, and also to provide a nice crunch. Alternatively, you can use Savoy or round cabbage. The paste can be prepared in advance and refrigerated; it will keep fresh and fragrant in the fridge for at least 3 days.

SERVES 4

2 tbsp vegetable oil
2 bay leaves
2 tbsp sweet soy sauce
1 tsp fine sea salt
1 tsp palm sugar or soft dark brown sugar
600g/1lb 5oz leg of lamb, cut into large chunks
100ml/3½fl oz/scant ½ cup coconut milk
200g/7oz pointed cabbage, cut into thick pieces
4 firm tomatoes, each cut into 8 pieces
2 spring onions, cut into pieces 2.5cm/1in long
4 kaffir lime leaves, ribs removed and thinly sliced
jasmine rice, to serve

FOR THE PASTE

2 banana shallots, peeled
3 garlic cloves, peeled
2.5cm/1in ginger
1 stalk of lemongrass, trimmed
3 red chillies, deseeded
1 tbsp ground coriander
½ tsp ground nutmeg

Blitz together the paste ingredients with 2 tablespoons of water using a handheld stick blender or food processor until fine and smooth.

Heat the oil in a large, deep saucepan over a medium heat and fry the bay leaves for 30 seconds, then stir in the paste and cook for 3 more minutes.

Next, stir in the soy sauce, salt and sugar, stir well and then add the lamb. Stir to coat the lamb and then add 200ml/7fl oz/scant 1 cup of water. Bring to the boil, reduce the heat and simmer uncovered for 20 minutes, or until the lamb is tender.

Add the coconut milk, stir well and then add the cabbage, tomatoes, spring onions and kaffir lime leaves. Continue to cook for 3 minutes until softened.

Turn off the heat and transfer to a large serving bowl. Serve with jasmine rice.

Braised Beef in Spices & Soy Sauce

The best beef dishes from Southeast Asia are always those that are simmered slowly with spices and herbs. As they say, this kind of dish always tastes better the next day. This recipe contains no chillies, but if you like a bit of heat, add slices of chilli when frying the paste ingredients.

SERVES 4

3 tbsp vegetable oil
2 red onions, thinly sliced
5cm/2in cinnamon stick
4 cloves
2 bay leaves
100ml/3½fl oz/scant ½ cup sweet soy sauce
2 tbsp light soy sauce
½ tbsp palm sugar
1 tsp fine sea salt
1 tbsp tamarind paste
800g/1lb 12oz beef rump, cut against the grain and into slices 2cm/¾in thick
2 large potatoes, about 400g/14oz, peeled and cut into medium chunks
2 medium tomatoes, each cut into 4 pieces
a handful of fresh coriander, for the garnish
rice, to serve

FOR THE PASTE

2 banana shallots, peeled
5 garlic cloves, peeled
2.5cm/1in ginger
1 tbsp ground coriander
1 tsp ground cumin
½ tsp ground nutmeg

Blitz together the paste ingredients with 2 tablespoons of water using a handheld stick blender or food processor until fine and smooth.

Heat the oil in a large, deep saucepan over a medium heat, and fry the onions until dark golden brown. Remove with a slotted spoon, dab with kitchen paper and set aside.

Using the remaining oil in the pan over a medium heat, add the cinnamon, cloves and bay leaves and cook for 30 seconds to infuse the oil.

Stir in the paste ingredients and cook for 2 minutes until fragrant. If the mixture is too dry, add a little extra oil to fry off the water in the paste and cook the paste thoroughly.

Add the sweet and light soy sauces, the sugar, salt and tamarind. Give the pan a good stir, add the beef and continue to cook for 2 minutes until the meat is sealed.

Next, add 300ml/10fl oz/1¼ cups of water and the potatoes and bring to the boil, then reduce the heat to low and simmer for 30 minutes, or until the beef is tender, stirring once or twice.

To finish, add the tomatoes and let them cook through; this should take about 2 minutes. Turn off the heat and serve in bowls with rice, garnished with the fried onions and coriander.

Beef & Bean Stir-fry

Cooking slices of beef in the Asian style can be tricky as it can easily become tough and chewy. A good tip is to sear the steak first, cut it into slices and then marinate with spices so the meat has a crust on the outside and is soft on the inside. Frying the kaffir lime leaves helps to infuse the oil, and you can use the leaves later as a garnish so the fragrance is retained. The lime leaves can be replaced with Thai basil leaves.

SERVES 2

1 tbsp vegetable oil, plus 1 tbsp extra
300g/10½oz beef steak (in one piece)
6 kaffir lime leaves, ribs removed and thinly sliced
3 garlic cloves, finely chopped
5cm/2in ginger, finely chopped
1 red chilli, deseeded and cut into thin strips
200g/7oz fine beans, both ends trimmed and cut into pieces 4cm/1½in long
1 tbsp tamarind paste, or juice of ½ lime
½ tbsp palm sugar
1 tbsp fish sauce
rice, to serve

FOR THE MARINADE

2 tsp coarsely crushed black pepper
1 tsp ground turmeric
½ tsp fine sea salt

Heat a heavy-based frying pan or skillet over a medium-high heat, pour in the ½ tablespoon of oil until the base of the pan is well covered. With a pair of tongs, sear and turn the steak for 2 minutes on each side or until it has a nice brown crust.

Transfer to a chopping board and cut into slices 2cm/¾in thick. Place in a medium bowl, together with the marinade ingredients, stir well and set aside for a minimum of 5 minutes. Wipe the pan clean with kitchen paper.

Heat the remaining 1 tablespoon of oil in the frying pan over a medium heat. Fry the kaffir lime leaves for 30 seconds and then lift them out onto a plate and dab with kitchen paper; set aside.

Using the same oil over a medium heat, fry the garlic, ginger and chilli for 1 minute or until the garlic has turned golden brown.

Stir in the beans, tamarind, sugar and fish sauce, together with 50ml/1¾fl oz/3 tbsp of water. Cook for 3 minutes or until the beans have wilted.

Add the beef, give the pan another good stir and turn off the heat. Transfer to two serving bowls with some rice, garnish with the lime leaves and serve.

Spicy Minced Beef & Kaffir Lime Leaves

Thai food is known for its spiciness, especially the use of bird's eye chillies. I have omitted these fiery chillies for this recipe and used chilli paste instead, because when my Thai friend Kym introduced me to this dish, the heat was too much for me – and I was too embarrassed to admit it! As I come from Malaysia I should be used to the heat, but my taste buds have changed. I am sure Kym won't be pleased to discover I have left out the chillies. If you like it hot, add either bird's eye or red chillies by slicing them thinly and frying them at the beginning with the onion, garlic and Thai basil. Kym served this dish with rice, as it should be, but here I serve it with baguettes as a perfect sandwich filling.

SERVES 4

1 tbsp vegetable oil
1 medium onion, diced
3 garlic cloves, finely chopped
10 fresh Thai basil leaves
500g/1lb 2oz minced beef
6 kaffir lime leaves, ribs removed, rolled and thinly sliced
2 French baguettes
1 round lettuce, cut in half and leaves picked
10 cherry tomatoes, halved

FOR THE SEASONING

2 tbsp chilli paste (I recommend sambal badjak)
1 tbsp light soy sauce, plus ½ tbsp extra for the salad dressing
2 tbsp oyster sauce
1 tbsp fish sauce
½ tbsp palm sugar

Mix the seasoning ingredients together well with 2 tablespoons of water in a small bowl.

Heat the oil in a wok or large frying pan over a medium-high heat and fry the onion, garlic and Thai basil for 2 minutes, until fragrant and golden.

Add the beef and seasoning mixture and cook for 5 minutes. Add the kaffir lime leaves, stir well and turn off the heat.

Cut each baguette lengthways and scoop out some of the insides to fit the filling inside. Fill each baguette with the beef mixture, lettuce and tomatoes. Cut each baguette in half, transfer to serving bowls and serve.

Beef in Spicy Soy Sauce

Sourcing a bottle of sweet soy sauce when I first arrived in the UK in 1994 was not easy. I made the sauce myself by simmering over a low heat 100ml/3½fl oz/scant ½ cup of dark soy sauce with 125g/4½oz/generous ½ cup dark muscovado sugar for 8 minutes. This should give 6–8 tablespoons of sweet soy sauce. Indonesian sweet soy sauce, known as *kecap manis*, is thicker than the Malaysian version. For a thicker sauce, continue to simmer for an additional 5 minutes.

SERVES 4

800g/1lb 12oz beef rump, cut into slices 2cm/¾in thick
1 tbsp black peppercorns, crushed
100ml/3½fl oz/scant ½ cup sweet soy sauce
50ml/1¾fl oz/3 tbsp dark soy sauce
2 tbsp vegetable oil
1 tsp fine sea salt
½ tbsp palm sugar
rice, to serve

FOR THE PASTE

3 red chillies, deseeded
3 garlic cloves, peeled
2 banana shallots, peeled
2.5cm/1in ginger
2.5cm/1in galangal, or ginger with 1 tsp lemon juice
3 stalks of lemongrass, trimmed

Marinade the beef with the black peppercorns and the sweet and dark soy sauces for 15 minutes.

Meanwhile, blitz together the paste ingredients with 2 tablespoons of water using a handheld stick blender or food processor until fine and smooth.

Heat the oil in a saucepan over a medium heat and fry the paste for 3 minutes.

Add the beef, together with the marinade, salt and sugar, stir well and continue to cook for 5 minutes to release the juices from the meat, then reduce the heat to medium-low and add 200ml/7fl oz/scant 1 cup of water.

Bring to the boil, then turn the heat down to low and simmer uncovered for 20–25 minutes until the beef is tender and the sauce has thickened.

Transfer to four serving bowls and serve with rice.

Chilli & Toasted Cumin Lamb Curry

Toasting the spices for this dish makes them even more fragrant as heating helps to release their aroma. I prefer to keep spice seeds in my kitchen cupboard and toast them before using, so a spice grinder is one of my must-have kitchen gadgets, apart from a traditional pestle and mortar for grinding smaller batches.

For shop-bought ground spices, it is best to store them in a cupboard as light makes them stale and they lose their aroma. For this Burmese dish, the cumin and mustard seeds that work so well with lamb, are toasted and left whole as the mustard seeds would be too overpowering if crushed.

SERVES 4

800g/1lb 12oz lamb shoulder or leg, fat trimmed and cut into slices 1cm/½in thick
1 tsp fine sea salt
1 tsp coarsely ground black pepper
1 tbsp cumin seeds
2 tsp black or brown mustard seeds
1 tbsp vegetable oil
3 garlic cloves, minced
1 courgette, about 200g/7oz, cut into 3cm/1¼in wedges
10 fresh mint leaves, for the garnish
1 red chilli, thinly sliced diagonally, for the garnish
rice, to serve

FOR THE SEASONING

2 tbsp chilli paste (I recommend sambal badjak)
3 tbsp dark soy sauce
1 tbsp rice vinegar
2 tsp palm sugar

Season the lamb with the salt and pepper.

In a small bowl, mix the seasoning ingredients well and set aside.

Heat a heavy-based frying pan over a medium heat and toast the cumin and mustard seeds for 1 minute until fragrant. Transfer to a small bowl.

Using the same pan, sear the lamb for 3 minutes, turning with a wooden spoon then stir in the oil and garlic and continue to cook for 1 minute.

Stir in the seasoning mixture and courgette, cook for 3 minutes until wilted and then turn off the heat.

Transfer to a serving bowl and garnish with the mint leaves and chilli. Serve with rice.

Maureen's Burmese Beef Curry

I was introduced to Maureen Duke by her son, Richard and his wife, Trisha. Maureen was born in Burma and came to London in 1952 with her husband intending just to stopover on their way to America, but in the event they stayed and started a family. Now in her eighties, Maureen is still cooking and she invited me to cook this dish in her kitchen. With her permission we went live on my Facebook page and the video was watched by over 100,000 people. Thank you Maureen for this wonderful memory and for sharing this recipe for us all to cook.

SERVES 4

2 banana shallots, peeled
5 garlic cloves, peeled
2.5cm/1in ginger
4 tbsp vegetable oil
2 stalks of lemongrass, white part only, thinly sliced
800g/1lb 12oz beef rump, cut into small chunks
2 tsp fine sea salt
rice, to serve

FOR THE SPICE PASTE

1½ tbsp ground paprika; use chilli powder if you prefer it spicy
2 tsp ground cumin
1 tbsp ground coriander
2 tsp ground turmeric
2 tbsp rice vinegar

Blitz together the shallots, garlic and ginger using a handheld stick blender or food processor into a fine, smooth paste.

Combine all the spice paste ingredients in a small bowl to make a smooth paste.

Heat the oil in a saucepan over a medium-high heat and cook the shallot mixture and lemongrass for 2 minutes until fragrant.

Next, add the spice paste and cook for 1 minute, then add the beef and salt, cook for 3 minutes to release the juices from the meat, and add 200ml/7fl/scant 1 cup of water.

Bring to the boil, reduce the heat to low and simmer for 20–30 minutes until the beef is nice and tender.

Turn off the heat and transfer to a serving bowl. Serve with rice.

Beef Wraps

The key to making a perfect roll depends on the wrapper being strong enough to hold the filling. I have frequently made the mistake of soaking the rice paper for too long and it has ended up becoming too soggy to roll.

For these rolls, my aim is to create a thick wrapper that holds the filling securely, and using three layers of rice paper seems to do the trick. In the method below, I share some tips on how to make a tight roll, and getting the timing right – it only takes 10 seconds for the rice paper to soften and be ready for rolling.

MAKES 8 ROLLS

600g/1lb 5oz beef steak, cut into 16 long strips, and about 5mm/¼in thick
1 tbsp light soy sauce
1 tbsp vegetable oil
24 pieces of rice paper, 22cm/8½in in diameter
2 Little Gem lettuces, leaves picked
1 carrot, cut into 8cm/3¼in sticks
1 cucumber, deseeded and cut into 8cm/3¼in sticks
salt and pepper

FOR THE DIPPING SAUCE

1 red chilli, deseeded and finely chopped
6 garlic cloves, minced
4 tbsp fish sauce
4 tbsp rice vinegar
2 tbsp palm sugar

FOR THE HERBS

24 fresh Thai basil leaves
24 fresh mint leaves
12 sprigs of fresh coriander, leaves picked

Rub the beef with salt, black pepper and the soy sauce. Set aside for 10 minutes to marinate.

To make the dipping sauce, mix together all the ingredients in a bowl with 100ml/3½fl oz/ scant ½ cup of warm water.

Heat the oil in a griddle pan or heavy-based frying pan over a high heat, sear the beef for 2 minutes on each side and then cut into strips.

Dip 3 pieces of rice paper simultaneously in a bowl of lukewarm water for 10 seconds, moving them around until they have softened, then drain on kitchen paper.

Making sure the pieces are layered on top of one another, place on a board and fold one-quarter of the rice paper inwards from the top.

Place a couple of lettuce leaves on top of the rice paper, leaving enough rice paper at the bottom to fold inwards. Two-thirds of the lettuce should be over the rice paper, with one-third left exposed at the top. This allows the wraps to hold the filling firmly. Add a few sticks of carrot and cucumber, two beef slices and then top with some of the herbs.

Starting with the bottom edge, turn the rice paper up over the filling, squeezing gently to make a tight package, then fold the left and right sides inwards. Repeat with the remaining wraps and filling. Arrange the rolls next to one another in a large, deep serving bowl, and serve immediately with the dipping sauce.

Beef Wraps p. 72

Padang Beef Sambal Stir-fry

For any beef recipe, I always recommend slicing rather than dicing the meat. This allows a greater surface area for the beef to absorb the marinade. Here I explain how to slice the beef perfectly at the correct thickness that allows time for the beef to become tender and nicely cooked with a full flavour. This recipe is adapted from the famous Padang dish, from the island of Sumatra in Indonesia. I marinated the beef with tamarind as its acidity is a perfect meat tenderizer. See page 14 for more on the best type of tamarind to use for all my recipes.

SERVES 4

2 x 250g/9oz sirloin beef steaks
1 tbsp light soy sauce
2 tbsp tamarind paste
1 tsp fine sea salt
1 tbsp vegetable oil
8 medium tomatoes, halved
2 white onions, cut into 1cm/½in rings
jasmine rice, to serve
2 spring onions, cut into thin strips for the garnish

FOR THE PASTE

5 garlic cloves, peeled
2.5cm/1in ginger
½ tbsp ground coriander
1 banana shallot, peeled
3 red chillies, deseeded
3 medium tomatoes, deseeded
½ tbsp palm sugar or soft light brown sugar
4 kaffir lime leaves, ribs removed, or the zest of 1 lime
1 tbsp rice vinegar

Put the beef on a chopping board, angle your knife to 45 degrees and cut into slices 1cm/½in thick. Transfer to a large bowl, add the soy sauce, tamarind and salt, give everything a good mix and set aside for 10 minutes to marinate.

Meanwhile, blitz together the paste ingredients using a handheld stick blender or food processor until fine and smooth.

Heat the oil in a wok or large frying pan over a medium heat. Add the beef, together with the marinade, and cook for 3 minutes to release the juices from the beef. Stir once or twice.

Next, add the paste and cook for 10 minutes, stirring every minute.

Add the tomatoes and onions, cook for 5 minutes until softened, stirring once or twice and then turn off the heat.

Spoon out into four serving bowls with some jasmine rice, garnish with the spring onions and serve.

Maureen's Burmese Chicken Curry

This is another great recipe I learned from the talented Maureen Duke, a great friend of mine who was born in Burma, and from whom I have learned a lot about Burmese cuisine. With her permission, I included this dish on my Southeast Asian Masterclasses menu, and I promised to share her inspiring story: When Maureen first arrived in London in 1952 she was unable to cook, but now she cooks and bakes passionately for her family and friends. She has a little notebook she keeps in the cupboard under the stairs with all her recipes neatly written down.

This curry works well if you want to cook a large batch and freeze in several food containers. If you prefer a less spicy version, replace the chilli powder with ground paprika. To save a bit of time, you can always blitz the onion, garlic and ginger together into a paste instead of chopping them finely.

SERVES 4

2 tsp ground turmeric
1 tbsp ground paprika
1 tbsp mild chilli powder
2 tbsp vegetable oil
2 medium onions, diced
5 garlic cloves, finely chopped
5cm/2in ginger, finely chopped
1 tbsp fish sauce
1 tsp fine sea salt
800g/1lb 12oz boneless chicken thighs, cut into large pieces
a handful of fresh coriander, leaves picked
rice, to serve

In a small bowl, mix the turmeric, paprika and chilli powder together well with 100ml/3½fl oz/scant ½ cup of water.

Heat the oil in a large, deep saucepan over a medium heat. Fry the onions, garlic and ginger for 3 minutes until fragrant.

Next, add the spice mixture, fish sauce and salt, cook for 1 minute and then add the chicken. Continue to cook for 2 more minutes and then stir in 200ml/7fl oz /scant 1 cup of water.

Bring to the boil, reduce the heat to low and simmer for 10 minutes until the chicken is cooked through, stirring once or twice.

Turn off the heat, transfer to a serving bowl and garnish with the coriander. Serve with rice.

Four-spice Chicken Curry

These four spices – cinnamon, star anise, cardamom and cloves – are known in Malaysian cooking as *empat sekawan* or 'four friends', as they are always added to curries for their complementary, aromatic flavours.

SERVES 4

2 tbsp vegetable oil
5cm/2in cinnamon stick
1 star anise
2 green cardamom pods, lightly bruised
3 cloves
1 banana shallot, finely chopped
3 garlic cloves, finely chopped
2.5cm/1in ginger, finely chopped
3 bay leaves
1 tbsp tamarind paste
1 tsp fine sea salt
1 tsp palm sugar
800g/1lb 12oz boneless chicken thighs, cut into small chunks
100ml/3½fl oz/scant ½ cup coconut milk
2 tomatoes, each cut into 8 pieces
3 sprigs of fresh coriander, finely chopped
rice, to serve

GROUND MIXED SPICES

½ teaspoon black or brown mustard seeds
2 tbsp ground coriander
½ tbsp ground cumin
½ tbsp ground fennel
2 tsp mild chilli powder
1 tsp ground turmeric

In a small bowl, thoroughly mix together the ground spices with 100ml/3½fl oz/scant ½ cup of water.

Heat the oil in a medium, deep saucepan over a medium heat. Stir in the cinnamon, star anise, cardamon and cloves and cook for 30 seconds until fragrant.

Add the shallot, garlic, ginger and bay leaves and cook for 3 minutes until golden brown, then add the ground spice mixture, tamarind, salt and sugar. Cook for 2 minutes.

Add the chicken and cook for 3 minutes to seal the meat, then add the coconut milk, together with 100ml/3½fl oz/scant ½ cup of water, bring to the boil and continue to cook over a medium heat for 8 minutes, stirring once or twice.

Add the tomatoes and cook for 2 minutes until softened. Transfer to a serving bowl and garnish with the coriander. Serve with rice.

The Night Market's Baked Chicken & Slaw

I have a vivid memory of saving my pocket money to buy this dish at the night market in my village when I was 11 years old. I waited all week for Friday night to come when the smoke from the stall carried with it the wonderful smell of grilled chicken that makes you instantly hungry.

At the night market, a half chicken would be flattened and tied lengthways onto bamboo sticks so it could be turned easily to cook both sides; for my version, I use a whole spatchcocked chicken, marinated in the sauce and baked in the oven.

SERVES 4

1 whole chicken, about 1.3kg/3lb, spatchcocked
2 tbsp vegetable oil
2 tbsp dark muscovado sugar
2 tsp fine sea salt

FOR THE MARINADE

2 banana shallots, peeled
3 garlic cloves, peeled
2.5cm/1in ginger
5cm/2in fresh turmeric, peeled, or 1 tsp ground turmeric
1 tbsp vegetable oil
1 tsp fine sea salt

FOR THE SLAW

50g/1¾oz/¼ cup white sugar
300g/10½oz red cabbage, thinly sliced
1 carrot, julienned
10 red radishes, thinly sliced
1 red onion, thinly sliced
1 cucumber, deseeded and julienned
100ml/3½fl oz/scant ½ cup rice vinegar

FOR THE SAUCE

3 banana shallots, peeled
3 garlic cloves, peeled
2.5cm/1in ginger
5 tbsp chilli paste (I recommend sambal badjak)
2 stalks of lemongrass, trimmed
2 tbsp coconut milk
1 tbsp tamarind paste

Preheat the oven to 160°C fan/180°C/gas mark 4.

Using a handheld stick blender or food processor, blitz together the marinade ingredients, apart from the salt, with 2 tablespoons of water until fine and smooth.

Rub the chicken with the 1 teaspoon of salt, then rub the chicken generously with the marinade and set aside in the fridge for 30 minutes or overnight.

For the slaw, dilute the sugar with 200ml/7fl oz/scant 1 cup of boiling water and then add all the other ingredients, give everything a good mix and set aside.

Meanwhile, blitz together the sauce ingredients with 2 tablespoons of water until fine and smooth. Heat the oil in a medium saucepan over a medium heat and cook the sauce for 3 minutes, then add the sugar and salt. Stir in 300ml/10fl oz/1¼ cups of water and bring to the boil, then reduce the heat to low and simmer for 10 minutes. Turn off the heat.

Lift the chicken out of the marinade, place on an oven tray and bake for 15 minutes. Discard the marinade. Take the chicken out of the oven, baste with the sauce and return to the oven for another 15 minutes. Repeat the same process once more (basting then baking the chicken) so the chicken has cooked for 45 minutes in total.

Give the baked chicken another baste once it has been removed from the oven. Cut into four pieces and divide between four serving bowls with the slaw on the side. Serve immediately with any remaining sauce alongside.

The Night Market's Baked Chicken & Slaw p. 80

'Pansuh' Baked Chicken

Traditionally, this Sarawakian dish from Borneo is cooked in a bamboo log. Chicken, shallots, garlic, ginger, galangal, lemongrass and chillies are wrapped in cassava leaves and stuffed inside the bamboo, which is then grilled on an open fire for 1 hour. My kitchen-friendly version uses baking paper to wrap all the ingredients with an outer layer of aluminium foil. I use kale and spinach instead of the nutty and earthy-flavoured cassava leaves.

SERVES 4

1kg/2lb 4oz boneless chicken thighs, cut into large pieces
100g/3½oz kale, roughly chopped
50g/1¾oz baby spinach
8 kaffir lime leaves, ribs removed and thinly sliced
1 tsp fine sea salt
½ tbsp coarsely ground black pepper
juice of 1 lime
jasmine rice, to serve

FOR THE PASTE

5 garlic cloves, peeled
2 banana shallots, peeled
5cm/2in ginger
3 stalks of lemongrass
5cm/2in galangal, or ginger with 2 tsp lemon juice
3 green chillies, deseeded

Preheat the oven to 160°C fan/180°C/gas mark 4.

Blitz together the paste ingredients with 2 tablespoons of water using a handheld stick blender or food processor until fine and smooth.

Transfer the paste into a large bowl and add all the other ingredients apart from the lime juice (and rice, to serve), mix well and set aside to marinate for 15 minutes.

Arrange a large sheet of aluminium foil with baking paper on top in a deep casserole dish or ovenproof bowl. Spoon the mixture onto the baking paper and wrap up in both sheets until properly sealed. Bake in the oven for 50 minutes.

Remove from the oven and allow to rest for 10 minutes; open up the foil and paper and squeeze over the lime juice. Give everything a good mix and transfer to a serving bowl. Serve with jasmine rice.

Honey & Chilli Grilled Chicken with Cucumber & Mango Ribbons

This is my favourite dish to prepare for friends at an outdoor barbeque but there is always the option to use the oven grill. I use the same dressing for the salad, which goes well with mango and julienned cucumber. You can always add blanched vermicelli noodles (about 200g/7oz) to the salad, which makes another great option.

SERVES 4

3 tbsp honey
2 tbsp fish sauce
1 tbsp rice vinegar
4 large chicken legs, skin on

FOR THE PASTE

6 garlic cloves, peeled
5cm/2in ginger
3 red chillies, deseeded
5 sprigs of fresh coriander
juice of 1 lime

FOR THE SALAD

1 unripe mango, peeled, stoned and sliced into ribbons with a peeler
1 cucumber, sliced into ribbons with a peeler
10 cherry tomatoes, halved
2 tbsp sweet chilli sauce
50g/1¾oz salted peanuts, coarsely crushed

Make the paste. Using a handheld stick blender or food processor, blitz together the garlic, ginger, chillies, coriander and lime juice, leaving the texture slightly coarse. Transfer to a small bowl and stir in the honey, fish sauce and rice vinegar. Mix well.

Place the chicken legs on a chopping board and score the skin about 2cm/¾in apart. Generously rub the paste over the chicken legs and leave to marinate for 30 minutes.

Preheat the oven to 160°C fan/180°C/gas mark 4. Place the chicken legs on an oven tray and bake the chicken for 1 hour, basting with the remaining marinade every 15 minutes until cooked through.

Before the final 15 minutes baking, turn the chicken and baste it again. Discard any remaining marinade.

Divide the baked chicken between four serving bowls, put the mango, cucumber and tomatoes on the side, topped with ½ tablespoon of sweet chilli sauce for each bowl and then scatter the peanuts on top. Serve immediately.

Chicken & Courgette 'Coconutless' Curry

Toasted rice powder, made of sticky rice, is very common in Thai and Lao cuisines for thickening up sauces, like cornflour in Chinese dishes. It also adds a roasted, smoky flavour to the dish. Thai curries are well-known for their use of coconut milk, but for this curry the paste is made just using fragrant herbs and spices. You can cook this dish with beef or make it a vegan dish with courgette, fennel, carrot and cabbage, replacing the fish sauce with soy sauce.

SERVES 4

3 tbsp fish sauce
1 tbsp palm sugar
2 tsp fine sea salt
800g/1lb 12oz boneless chicken thighs, cut into large pieces
3 green chillies, deseeded and cut in half lengthways
1 courgette, about 400g/14oz, cut in half lengthways and cut diagonally into slices 1cm/½in thick
2 tbsp toasted rice powder, see page 36
jasmine rice, to serve

FOR THE PASTE

1 banana shallot, peeled
3 garlic cloves, peeled
5cm/2in galangal, or ginger with 2 tsp lemon juice
2 stalks of lemongrass, trimmed
5cm/2in fresh turmeric, peeled, or 1 tsp ground turmeric

FOR THE GARNISH

10 sprigs of fresh dill, roughly chopped
10 sprigs of fresh coriander, roughly chopped
10 fresh Thai basil leaves
4 kaffir lime leaves, ribs removed and thinly sliced

Blitz together all the paste ingredients with 2 tablespoons of water using a handheld stick blender or food processor until fine and smooth.

Bring 700ml/24fl oz/2¾ cups of water to the boil in a large saucepan and add the paste, together with the fish sauce, sugar and salt. Continue to cook over a medium heat for 2 minutes, then stir in the chicken and cook for 8 minutes or until the chicken is cooked through.

Stir in the chillies and courgette, cook for 2 minutes until wilted, then add the toasted rice powder and continue to cook for 2 minutes. Turn off the heat and transfer to a serving bowl.

Mix together all the herbs for the garnish and sprinkle over the top. Serve with jasmine rice.

Chicken Adobo

As simple as can be, this dish provides a wonderful blend of soy sauce, vinegar and peppery heat from the crushed black peppercorns. Adobo has always been a favourite of mine that I kept asking my Filipino friends in Manchester to cook for me.

When you talk to Pinoys – what people from the Philippines call themselves – and tell them that you love and know how to cook Adobo, their faces light up and they get excited that you are honouring what they consider to be their national dish. The black peppercorns taste even better if you crush them just before cooking.

SERVES 4

800g/1lb 12oz boneless chicken thighs, cut into 4cm/1½in cubes
5 garlic cloves, finely chopped
100ml/3½fl oz/scant ½ cup dark soy sauce
2 tbsp rice vinegar
2 tbsp vegetable oil
3 bay leaves, bruised
1 banana shallot, finely chopped
½ tbsp palm sugar or soft light brown sugar
1 tbsp black peppercorns, coarsely crushed
1 spring onion, cut into thin strips and soaked in cold water until curled, then drained
rice, to serve

In a large bowl, marinate the chicken with the garlic, soy sauce and vinegar for 10 minutes.

Heat the oil in a large saucepan over a medium heat. Add the bay leaves and stir for 30 seconds to infuse the oil.

Next, add the shallot and cook for 3 minutes until golden brown, then stir in the chicken without the marinade, and cook for 3 minutes until the chicken has browned.

Next, stir in the marinade, sugar and black pepper, mixing well.

Stir in 200ml/7fl oz/scant 1 cup of water, bring to the boil, then reduce the heat to low and simmer for 20 minutes. Turn the chicken halfway through cooking. After 20 minutes the sauce should have reduced and thickened up.

Turn the heat off, divide the chicken adobo between four serving bowls, garnish with the spring onion and serve with rice.

Kalio Chicken Curry

If you enjoy the popular dish Rendang, either with chicken or beef, Kalio will certainly be another favourite. The sauce is thick and creamy, not dry like Rendang, but the flavour is almost the same, except that it contains no toasted coconut and is also quicker to cook.

SERVES 4

2 tbsp vegetable oil
2 tbsp tamarind paste
1½ tsp fine sea salt
½ tbsp palm sugar
1kg/2lb 4oz boneless chicken thighs, cut into large pieces
200ml/7fl oz/scant 1 cup coconut milk
6 kaffir lime leaves, ribs removed and thinly sliced
jasmine rice, to serve

FOR THE PASTE

1 banana shallot, peeled
3 garlic cloves, peeled
2.5cm/1in ginger
2 stalks of lemongrass, trimmed
5cm/2in galangal, or ginger with 2 tsp lemon juice
3 red chillies, deseeded
5cm/2in fresh turmeric, peeled, or 1 tsp ground turmeric

Blitz together the paste ingredients with 2 tablespoons of water using a handheld stick blender or food processor until fine and smooth.

Heat the oil in a large, deep saucepan over a medium heat and cook the paste for 2 minutes until fragrant.

Next, add the tamarind, salt and sugar, continue to cook for 1 minute and then stir in the chicken. Cook for 3 minutes to seal and then stir in the coconut milk, together with 200ml/7fl oz/scant 1 cup of water. Bring to the boil, reduce the heat to medium-low and simmer, uncovered, for 20 minutes, stirring every 5 minutes.

Next, add the kaffir lime leaves, give everything a good stir and turn off the heat. Divide the curry between four serving bowls, and serve with jasmine rice.

Chicken & Black Pepper Stir-fry

For stir-fry dishes, I prefer to use chicken breast; for curries and stews, I use chicken thighs as the longer cooking time does not make the meat tough.

When using chicken breast, I slice the meat instead of dicing it, as this provides more surface area for the pieces to absorb the sauce. I also cut beans diagonally for the same reason. This simple stir-fry dish has strong garlic and pepper flavours that complement one another well. You can leave the chilli out to make it less spicy, and as well as rice, this dish is also great served with egg noodles.

SERVES 4

1 tbsp vegetable oil
5 garlic cloves, finely chopped
2.5cm/1in ginger, finely chopped
1 green chilli, deseeded and thinly sliced
600g/1lb 5oz chicken breast fillets, cut into slices 2cm/¾in thick
2 tbsp sweet soy sauce
½ tbsp black peppercorns, lightly crushed
2 tbsp oyster sauce
150g/5½oz fine beans, both ends trimmed and cut diagonally into pieces 4cm/1½in long
1 carrot, about 150g/5½oz, peeled, cut in half lengthways and sliced diagonally into pieces 5mm/¼in thick
½ tsp fine sea salt
2 spring onions, cut into thin strips and soaked in cold water until curled, then drained
jasmine rice or egg noodles, to serve

Heat the oil in a wok or large frying pan over a medium-high heat and fry the garlic, ginger and chilli for 2 minutes or until turning a nice light golden brown.

Next, add the chicken, soy sauce and black pepper. Cook for 3 minutes until the chicken pieces are sealed and about half-cooked.

Next, add the oyster sauce, beans, carrot and salt with 100ml/3½fl oz/scant ½ cup of water and cook for 5 more minutes, with the lid on, until the chicken is cooked through.

Turn off the heat and spoon the stir-fry into four serving bowls with some jasmine rice or egg noodles. Garnish with the spring onions.

Lombok Grilled Chicken

I remember eating this dish on a holiday in Lombok, Indonesia, just a week before Mount Agung erupted in Bali in 2019; the volcano can be seen from Lombok island. I learned this recipe from Ani, who had set up a café outside her home where we were eating. She was alone in the kitchen as her husband was working a night shift. The café suddenly became very busy and Ani allowed me to assist her. As a result, I learned a few Lombok recipes that have been included in this book with her permission. I never thought my holiday would turn into a learning opportunity and I am very grateful to Ani for letting me share her recipes.

SERVES 4

2 tbsp vegetable oil
1 tsp fine sea salt
1 tbsp palm sugar or soft light brown sugar
2 tbsp tamarind paste
1kg/2lb 4oz boneless chicken thighs, cut into large pieces
10 sprigs of fresh coriander, leaves picked
jasmine rice, to serve

FOR THE PASTE

1 banana shallot, peeled
3 garlic cloves, peeled
2.5cm/1in ginger
2 large tomatoes, deseeded
3 red chillies, deseeded
1 tsp shrimp paste

Blitz together the paste ingredients using a handheld stick blender or food processor until fine and smooth.

Heat the oil in a large frying pan over a medium heat and fry the paste for 3 minutes until fragrant. Add the salt, sugar and tamarind. Cook for 1 minute, then add the chicken and continue to cook for a further 2 minutes to coat the chicken with the paste.

Next, stir in 200ml/7fl oz/scant 1 cup of water, bring to the boil then reduce the heat to low and simmer for 15 minutes, turning the chicken halfway through cooking. The sauce should have reduced and thickened up.

Preheat the grill to maximum. Transfer the chicken to an oven tray and grill for 5–8 minutes so the pieces are nicely charred. Divide the chicken between four serving bowls and serve with jasmine rice.

Baked Chicken

My version of this Lombok dish is to oven bake the chicken pieces instead of grilling. Cooking the chicken in the paste and its own juices makes it soft and tender. The technique of removing the aluminium foil after the dish has been in the oven for 20 minutes helps to stop the top of the chicken from getting burned, but allows it to become charred and slightly crispy.

SERVES 4

1kg/2lb 4oz boneless chicken thighs, cut into large pieces
1 tsp fine sea salt
2 tbsp vegetable oil, plus extra for brushing
2 garlic bulbs, sliced in half
10 fresh mint leaves, roughly chopped
jasmine rice, to serve

FOR THE PASTE

2 banana shallots, peeled
3 garlic cloves, peeled
5cm/2in ginger
3 green chillies, deseeded
1 tsp shrimp paste
½ tbsp palm sugar
1 tbsp tamarind paste

Preheat the oven to 160°C fan/180°C/gas mark 4.

Blitz together the paste ingredients with 2 tablespoons of water using a handheld stick blender or food processor until fine and smooth.

In a casserole dish or ovenproof bowl, season the chicken pieces with the salt and set aside.

Heat the oil in a small frying pan and sauté the paste for 2 minutes, then transfer to the casserole dish and mix well with the chicken. Marinate for 10 minutes.

Put the garlic bulbs in between the chicken pieces and brush the chicken and garlic with some extra oil. Cover the dish with aluminium foil and bake for 50 minutes, removing the foil after the dish has been in the oven for 20 minutes.

Remove from the oven and garnish with the mint leaves. Serve with jasmine rice.

Seared Duck in Massaman Curry

I first tried this duck dish at a Thai restaurant in the early 2000s after moving to London, and since then it has become one of my favourite Thai dishes. The rich, nutty flavour of the curry paste blends well with the duck, but what made the curry memorable was that the duck was seared until crispy on the outside and tender on the inside; if you prefer your duck to be fully cooked, simmer over a low heat for 30 minutes. I cook the curry sauce first and sear the duck afterwards.

SERVES 4

2 tbsp vegetable oil
4 boneless duck breasts (skin on)
3 green cardamom pods, lightly bruised
3 cloves
5cm/2in cinnamon stick
1 tsp fine sea salt
1 tbsp palm sugar
1 tbsp tamarind paste
1 tbsp fish sauce
200ml/7fl oz/scant 1 cup coconut milk
400g/14oz peeled baby potatoes
3 tbsp frozen peas
1 tbsp salted peanuts
salt and pepper

FOR THE PASTE

3 red chillies, deseeded
1 banana shallot, peeled
5 garlic cloves, peeled
2 stalks of lemongrass, trimmed
2.5cm/1in galangal, or ginger with 1 tsp lemon juice
10 sprigs of fresh coriander
1 tbsp ground coriander
1 tsp ground cumin
½ tsp ground nutmeg
50g/1¾oz/ ½ cup ready-salted peanuts

Preheat the oven to 160°C fan/180°C/gas mark 4.

Blitz together the paste ingredients with 2 tablespoons of water using a handheld stick blender or food processor until fine and smooth.

For the duck, heat ½ tablespoon of oil in a large, heavy-based ovenproof frying pan over a high heat.

Place the duck breasts, skin-side down, in the pan and season the other (uppermost) side with salt and pepper. Cook for 3 minutes or until most of the fat has run out into the pan and the skin is golden brown.

Turn the duck over and cook for 1 minute, then transfer the pan to the oven and cook for 7 minutes. Remove from the oven and allow to rest on a board, covered with foil, for 10 minutes and then cut into slices 2cm/¾in thick.

Meanwhile, for the sauce, heat the remaining oil in a separate saucepan over a medium-high heat and add the cardamom, cloves and cinnamon, cook for 30 seconds to infuse the oil and then stir in the paste.

Cook for 2 minutes, then add the salt, sugar, tamarind and fish sauce, give the pan a good stir and add the coconut milk, potatoes and peas, together with 200ml/7fl oz/scant 1 cup of water.

Bring to the boil, reduce the heat to low and simmer for 10–15 minutes until the potatoes are cooked through.

Place the duck into a large serving bowl and pour over the sauce. Garnish with the peanuts.

Five-spice Duck & Kailan Stir-fry

My friend Eric from Delft in the Netherlands introduced me to this simple dish. It was his first time cooking for me and, like many of my friends, he was anxious about cooking for me in case I criticized his food, which is something I would never do. In fact, I really look forward to the times when other people cook for me as it makes a welcome change, and I honestly have no expectations. This recipe differs slightly from Eric's as I combine oyster sauce and sweet soy sauce to give a slight sweetness to the dish. You can replace the kailan (Chinese broccoli) with pak choi as an alternative.

SERVES 2

2 tsp five-spice powder
2 small boneless duck breasts (skin on)
½ tbsp vegetable oil
3 garlic cloves, finely chopped
300g/10½oz kailan (Chinese broccoli), stems cut in half lengthways
3 tbsp oyster sauce
1 tbsp sweet soy sauce
1 tsp sesame oil
½ tbsp toasted sesame seeds
salt and pepper
jasmine rice, to serve

Preheat the oven to 160°C fan/180°C/gas mark 4.

Rub the five-spice on both sides of the duck breasts and season with salt and pepper.

Heat the vegetable oil in a large, heavy-based frying pan over a medium-high heat. Place the duck breasts, skin-side down, in the pan and cook for about 3 minutes, or until the skin is golden brown and the fat has run out into the pan. Turn the duck over and cook for 1 more minute. Turn off the heat and transfer the duck to an oven tray and cook in the oven for 7 minutes for medium-rare, then take it out to rest for 5 minutes, covered with aluminium foil.

Meanwhile, use 1 tablespoon of the remaining fat from the duck in the frying pan and place over a medium-high heat. Stir in the garlic and cook for 30 seconds, then add the kailan, oyster sauce and sweet soy sauce. Give the pan a good stir, cover with a lid and cook for 2 minutes until wilted. Add the sesame oil, give everything another stir and then turn off the heat. Transfer the kailan to a large serving bowl without the sauce and leave a space in the bowl for the rice.

Slice the duck into strips and place on top of the kailan. Drizzle over the sauce and garnish with the sesame seeds. Add the rice to the bowl and serve at once.

Curries

& Stir-fries

Vegetarian & Plant-based

Tempeh, Cabbage & Bean Stir-fry

This is a quick stir-fry dish using my reverse cooking method where the sauce mixture is added at the end; this allows the vegetables to cook nicely and retain their crunch. The Chinese cabbage can be replaced with Savoy or white cabbage.

For the chilli oil I use the brand Lao Gan Ma, which is mild and comes with crispy chilli flakes. Reduce the quantity if you are using spicy chilli oil. If sourcing tempeh (see page 17) is not possible where you live, replace with firm tofu and cut into 3cm/1¼in cubes. Follow the same method for frying the tofu as for the tempeh below.

SERVES 4

1 Chinese cabbage, about 600g/1lb 5oz
2 tbsp chilli oil
2 tbsp sweet soy sauce
2 tsp sesame oil
3 tbsp vegetable oil
200g/7oz tempeh, cut into slices 1cm/½in thick
3 garlic cloves, thinly sliced
1 banana shallot, thinly sliced into rings
1 courgette, about 300g/10½oz, cut lengthways and into slices 1cm/½in thick
200g/7oz fine beans, both ends trimmed and cut diagonally into pieces 4cm/1½in long
1 tsp fine sea salt
jasmine rice, to serve

On a chopping board, slice the cabbage into quarters lengthways and cut off the stem. Next, cut each quarter into strips 2cm/¾in wide. Transfer to a colander and rinse well, set aside.

In a small bowl, add the chilli oil, soy sauce and sesame oil and mix well.

Heat the vegetable oil in a wok or large frying pan over a medium-high heat. Fry the tempeh in batches for 2 minutes on each side until brown and crispy. Transfer to a bowl with a slotted spoon and dab away any excess oil with kitchen paper.

Using the remaining oil, left in the pan over a medium heat, fry the garlic and shallot for 2 minutes until golden brown.

Next, add the courgette, beans and salt, cover the wok or frying pan with a lid and cook for 3 minutes. Open the lid and add the cabbage, cook for 3 more minutes with the lid on, stirring every minute until the cabbage has wilted. Stir in the sauce mixture and cook for 1 minute, then stir in the tempeh. Give the pan another good stir and cook for a further minute.

Turn off the heat and transfer to a serving bowl. Serve with jasmine rice.

Tofu & Oyster Mushroom Curry

Tofu is a good source of plant-based protein. It is made of soya, which is curdled and made into a solid block and it comes in a variety of textures, from silken to extra firm tofu. For this recipe, I recommend you use firm tofu and don't stir the dish too frequently, to stop the tofu from breaking up. This creamy curry is heavily infused with lemongrass and turmeric and is best served with rice or vermicelli noodles.

SERVES 4

400ml/14fl oz/1¾ cups coconut milk
6 kaffir lime leaves, ribs removed and thinly sliced
2 tsp fine sea salt
½ tbsp palm sugar
2 tbsp tamarind paste
300g/10½oz oyster mushrooms, halved for any larger mushrooms
400g/14oz firm tofu, drained cut into 2cm/¾in cubes
4 sprigs of fresh coriander, for the garnish
1 red chilli, deseeded and thinly sliced, for the garnish
rice or vermicelli noodles, to serve

FOR THE PASTE

1 banana shallot, peeled
3 garlic cloves, peeled
3 stalks of lemongrass, trimmed
5cm/2in fresh turmeric, peeled, or 1 tsp ground turmeric

Blitz together the paste ingredients with 2 tablespoons of water using a handheld stick blender or food processor until fine and smooth.

Put the coconut milk and kaffir lime leaves into a saucepan, bring to the boil, reduce the heat to low and simmer for 2 minutes.

Stir in the paste, salt, sugar and tamarind and cook for 1 minute, then stir in the mushrooms and tofu, together with 200ml/7fl oz/scant 1 cup of water. Stir gently once or twice without breaking up the tofu. Cook for 3 minutes or until the mushrooms have softened.

Turn the heat off and transfer to four serving bowls with some rice or vermicelli noodles. Garnish with the coriander and chilli and serve.

Butternut Squash, Green Pea & Chickpea Curry

Many dishes in this book I recommend serving with rice or noodles. This dish, however, is an exception as I prefer to have it with naan bread that has been slightly warmed so that it is soft and easier to tear for dipping in the curry.

You can always replace the squash with pumpkin or sweet potato. This curry is suitable for cooking in large batches for freezing and will keep for at least a couple of months.

SERVES 4

2 tbsp vegetable oil
5cm/2in cinnamon stick
1 star anise
1 banana shallot, finely chopped
3 garlic cloves, finely chopped
2.5cm/1in ginger, finely chopped
1 tsp palm sugar or soft light brown sugar
1 tsp fine sea salt
2 tbsp tamarind paste
1 x 400g/14oz can chickpeas, rinsed and drained
600g/1lb 5oz butternut squash, peeled, deseeded and cut into bite-sized chunks
100g/3½oz frozen peas
200ml/7fl oz/scant 1 cup coconut milk
10 sprigs of fresh parsley, roughly chopped
naan bread or jasmine rice, to serve

FOR THE GROUND MIXED SPICES

1½ tbsp ground coriander
2 tsp ground cumin
1 tsp ground fennel
1½ tsp mild chilli powder, or ground paprika if you prefer it less spicy
1 tsp ground turmeric

In a small bowl, mix the ground spices with 100ml/3½fl oz/scant ½ cup of water. Set aside.

Heat the oil in a large saucepan over a medium heat. Add the cinnamon and star anise and cook for 30 seconds to infuse the oil.

Next, stir in the shallot, garlic and ginger and cook for 2 minutes until fragrant.

Add the ground spice mixture, sugar, salt and tamarind. Cook for 2 minutes, then stir in the chickpeas and butternut squash and cook for 1 minute, stirring constantly to coat with the spice mixture.

Next, add 400ml/14fl oz/1¾ cups of water and bring to the boil. Carry on cooking for 10 minutes over a medium-low heat, stirring once or twice. Check the squash has softened, then add the peas and coconut milk, bring back to the boil once again and cook for 2 minutes to allow the coconut to combine with the curry mixture.

Turn off the heat, transfer to small serving bowls and garnish with the parsley. Serve with warmed naan bread or jasmine rice.

Jackfruit & Sweet Potato Rendang with Cucumber Relish

I adapted this recipe from my late mother's chicken rendang recipe, which I called a 'lazy' rendang – she never knew that, of course. Unlike cooking the usual curries where the ingredients are added in stages, this dish only requires 3 minutes to initally sauté the paste ingredients so that the chillies are cooked properly, followed by the rest of the ingredients, then toasted coconut and kaffir lime leaves are added last.

SERVES 4

200g/7oz block of creamed coconut, sleeve removed and cut into small pieces
2 tbsp vegetable oil
1 x 565g/20oz can jackfruit in brine, drained and rinsed
400g/14oz sweet potatoes, peeled and cut into 5cm/2in chunks
½ tbsp palm sugar
1½ tsp fine sea salt
1 tbsp tamarind paste
400ml/14fl oz/1¾ cups coconut milk
6 kaffir lime leaves, ribs removed and thinly sliced
rice, to serve

FOR THE PASTE

2 banana shallots, peeled
3 garlic cloves, peeled
2.5cm/1in ginger
2.5cm/1in galangal, or ginger with 1 tsp lime juice
2 stalks of lemongrass, trimmed
3 red chillies, deseeded
5cm/2in fresh turmeric, peeled, or 1 tsp ground turmeric

FOR THE RELISH

2 tbsp white sugar
4 tbsp rice vinegar
1 medium cucumber, thinly sliced
1 red onion, cut in half and thinly sliced
1 red chilli, deseeded and cut into thin, diagonal slices

Blitz together the paste ingredients with 2 tablespoons of water using a handheld stick blender until fine and smooth.

In a small frying pan and over a medium-low heat, cook the creamed coconut pieces for 4–5 minutes, constantly stirring with a spatula or flat wooden spoon. Cook until light brown and remove from the heat immediately as the residual heat will carry on cooking the coconut. The colour will change to dark brown once it has been set aside for a few minutes. It is important that the coconut does not burn otherwise it will turn bitter.

Heat the oil in a large saucepan over a medium-high heat and cook the paste for 3 minutes until fragrant.

Stir in all the other ingredients, apart from the toasted coconut and kaffir lime leaves, together with 200ml/7fl oz/scant 1 cup of water, bring to the boil, then reduce the heat to low and let it simmer for 15 minutes, stirring occasionally. This will thicken the sauce and the sweet potatoes will turn soft and mushy.

Add the toasted coconut and kaffir lime leaves, cook for a further 2 minutes, then turn off the heat.

For the relish, in a medium bowl, mix the sugar with 200ml/7fl oz/scant 1 cup of lukewarm water. Stir in the vinegar, cucumber, onion and chilli. Set aside for 5 minutes before serving.

Serve the rendang with rice and the relish on the side.

'Kacang Pool' Three-bean Stew

There is a wonderful tale about how the dish known as *ful medames*, which originated in Egypt, migrated to Johor, a state in southern Malaysia. The late Sultan of Johor, Sultan Abu Bakar, who travelled extensively during his life and reign, especially to Europe in the late 19th century, brought back and introduced the dish to his people, and since then it has become a local favourite. The Johorean dish *kacang pool* has been adapted to use locally sourced ingredients. My vegetarian version uses poached eggs and is served with bread rolls, unlike the original version that is cooked with minced meat and served with slices of soft white bread. For the curry powder, Malaysian curry powder is best, but Madras curry powder works well too.

SERVES 4

2 tbsp curry powder (see intro)
½ tsp ground white pepper
1 tsp ground cumin
1 tbsp ground coriander
1 tsp ground paprika
1 tbsp tomato purée
1 tbsp tamarind paste
2 tbsp unsalted butter
1 shallot, finely chopped
3 garlic cloves, finely chopped
3 sprigs of fresh parsley, roughly chopped, plus extra for the garnish
1 x 300g/10½oz can broad beans in water, drained
1 x 400g/14oz can red kidney beans in water, drained and lightly mashed
400ml/14fl oz/1¾ cups vegetable stock
1 tsp palm sugar or soft light brown sugar
1 tsp fine sea salt
1 x 415g/14½oz can baked beans
4 eggs
4 bread rolls, to serve

In a small bowl, mix the curry powder, white pepper, cumin, coriander, paprika, tomato purée and tamarind paste together well.

Heat the butter in a large saucepan over a medium heat and fry the shallot, garlic and parsley for 2 minutes until golden brown.

Next, add the curry powder and ground spice mixture, cook for 30 seconds and then stir in 100ml/3½fl oz/scant ½ cup of water. Cook for 2 minutes and stir once or twice.

Next, add the broad beans, kidney beans, vegetable stock, sugar and salt. Bring to the boil, reduce the heat to low and cook for 5 minutes, stirring once or twice.

Add the baked beans, continue to cook for 2 minutes, then make four well-spaced depressions in the mixture and crack an egg into each one. Place a piece of aluminium foil over the pan to trap the steam and cover with a lid. Cook for 6 minutes and then check to see if the eggs are nicely poached. If the eggs are still not set, continue to cook for a further 2 minutes.

Turn off the heat, then using a ladle, gently transfer the mixture into four serving bowls, garnish with extra parsley and serve with the bread rolls.

Plant-based Crispy Pancake

When I lived in Manchester, I often visited a local Vietnamese restaurant, which is where I discovered this crispy pancake. I ordered this dish many times but had no idea I was eating it incorrectly until the waiting staff pointed it out. The pancake should be cut or torn into a bite-sized piece, rolled up with the lettuce and fresh herbs and then dipped in the sauce. I had been eating it with a knife and fork like a normal pancake, but it is much more fun to use your fingers! Replace the fish sauce with light soy sauce for a vegan dipping sauce.

MAKES 8

½ tbsp vegetable oil, plus ½ tbsp extra
1 large yellow pepper, deseeded and cut into strips
1 red onion, sliced
2 large pickled beetroots, drained and thinly sliced
6 pickled gherkins, drained and thinly sliced lengthways
2 tomatoes, thinly sliced
150g/5½oz bean sprouts
1 round lettuce, leaves separated
a handful of fresh coriander
a handful of fresh mint
a handful of fresh Thai basil

FOR THE PANCAKE BATTER

100g/3½oz/xx cup rice flour
1 tsp ground turmeric
200ml/7fl oz/scant 1 cup coconut milk
1 tsp fine sea salt
1 spring onion, cut into 5mm/¼in thick slices

FOR THE DIPPING SAUCE

2 tbsp fish sauce
3 garlic cloves, finely chopped
1 tbsp palm sugar
juice of 1 lime
1 tbsp rice vinegar

Heat the oil in a large frying pan over a medium-high heat and fry the yellow pepper for 2 minutes until softened, then transfer to a plate using a slotted spoon. Using the same pan, pour in the remaining oil and fry the onion for 1 minute until softened. Transfer to the plate with the pepper.

Place all the ingredients for the pancake batter in a bowl, together with 200ml/7fl oz/scant 1 cup of water, and mix well.

Heat a non-stick frying pan over a medium-low heat, ladle in a thin layer of batter and tilt the pan to cover the entire base of the pan and create a thin pancake. On one side of the pancake, add one-eighth of the pepper, onion, beetroots, gherkins and tomatoes, then top with a handful of bean sprouts and cover with a lid. Cook for 2 minutes, then lift the lid and continue to cook for 1 more minute.

Fold the pancake in half, transfer to a serving bowl and garnish with some of the lettuce and herbs. Repeat for the remaining batter and filling to make eight filled pancakes in total.

Combine all the dipping sauce ingredients in a small bowl. Serve the pancakes with the dipping sauce on the side.

Tofu in Tomato Sauce

Choosing the right tofu for a stir-fry dish is important so that it does not break up in the sauce. I always go for firm tofu and lightly fry it so it is crispy on the outside and soft on the inside. This helps to make the tofu more robust so it will not break up in the sauce. You can also brush the tofu pieces with vegetable oil and bake in the oven at 160°C fan/180°C/gas mark 4 for 15 minutes to achieve the same effect. Whichever method you use, season it with salt and pepper to enhance the flavour.

SERVES 4

2 tbsp vegetable oil
600g/1lb 5oz firm tofu, drained and cut into 3cm/1¼in cubes
3 garlic cloves, finely chopped
1 red chilli, deseeded and thinly sliced, half for cooking and the other half for the garnish
1 medium onion, diced
3 medium ripe tomatoes, diced
1 tbsp tomato purée
½ tsp fine sea salt
½ tsp palm sugar or soft light brown sugar
1 tbsp light soy sauce
1 spring onion, cut into 5cm/2in pieces, thinly sliced and soaked in cold water until curled, then drained
10 sprigs of fresh coriander, leaves picked
salt and pepper
rice, to serve

Using a non-stick frying pan, heat the oil over a medium-low heat and fry the tofu for 6–8 minutes until golden brown. Season with salt and pepper. Using a slotted spoon, transfer the tofu to a plate lined with kitchen paper and dab away any excess oil. Cook in two batches if the frying pan is too small to cook all the pieces in one go.

Using the same pan, and with the remaining oil in the pan, increase the heat to medium-high. Cook the garlic and half of the sliced chilli for 30 seconds, then stir in the onion and cook for 3 minutes until golden brown. Next, add the tomatoes, tomato purée, salt, sugar and soy sauce, cook for 1 minute and then stir in 200ml/7fl oz/scant 1 cup of water. Bring to the boil, reduce the heat and simmer for 3 minutes.

Add the tofu, cook for 3 more minutes and gently stir the dish once or twice.

Turn off the heat, transfer to a serving bowl and garnish with the spring onion, coriander and the remaining chilli. Serve with rice.

Wok-fried Sweet Potato & Beans in Satay Sauce

This is my 'cheat' version of satay sauce that uses a peanut butter containing 100 per cent peanuts. It works much better as it avoids having to prepare peanuts from scratch. I cook this dish for my Dutch friends and they absolutely love it as peanut butter is a great favourite in the Netherlands. The shops there carry a good selection of peanut butter and the one I used for this recipe comes with large pieces of nut. It is unusual to see sweet potato in a stir-fry; when it does appear it is generally pre-cooked. For this dish, everything is cooked together, which allows the sweet potato to absorb all the flavour of the lemongrass. You can replace the sweet potato with pumpkin, when it is in season, or with butternut squash, which is another great alternative.

For the chilli paste I use sambal badjak, but you can replace this with sweet chilli sauce and omit the palm sugar.

SERVES 4

600g/1lb 5oz sweet potatoes
2 tbsp vegetable oil
1 medium onion, diced
3 garlic cloves, finely chopped
1 stalk of lemongrass, white part only, thinly sliced
150g/5½oz fine beans, both ends trimmed, cut diagonally into 4cm/1½in pieces
rice, to serve

FOR THE SAUCE MIXTURE

½ tbsp chilli paste (I recommend sambal badjak)
½ tbsp sweet soy sauce
2 tbsp good-quality crunchy peanut butter
2 tbsp coconut milk
1 tbsp tamarind paste
½ tbsp palm sugar
1 tsp fine sea salt

Peel the sweet potatoes, cut in half lengthways and then cut into slices 1cm/½in thick. Soak in cold water for 10 minutes and then drain. Pat dry with kitchen paper.

In a small bowl, mix the sauce ingredients together with 100ml/3½fl oz/scant ½ cup of water and set aside.

Heat the oil in a wok over a medium heat and fry the onion, garlic and lemongrass for 3 minutes, stirring once or twice. Next, stir in the sweet potatoes and cook for 1 minute, then add 200ml/7fl oz/scant 1 cup of water, cover and cook for 4 minutes, stirring every minute. Next, add the beans and sauce mixture and cook for 3 minutes until the beans have wilted. Transfer to four serving bowls and serve with rice.

Thom Kha Soup with Charred Vegetables

For this recipe, I prefer to make my own stock infused with Asian herbs instead of shop-bought stock cubes that mainly consist of Western herbs. This coconut-based soup is usually served as a starter in many Thai restaurants, but in Thailand itself it is served as a side dish, together with other main dishes, as the locals love to have all the dishes served at once. Galangal is the main ingredient, which gives the citrusy flavour, but if sourcing it is difficult where you live, adding ginger with a little lemon juice does the trick. For this dish, I recommend serving it with vermicelli noodles, if you would like an accompaniment.

SERVES 4

200ml/7fl oz/scant 1 cup coconut milk
½ tbsp palm sugar
1 tsp fine sea salt
1 lime, halved, one half for the juice, the other cut into 4 wedges
½ tbsp vegetable oil, plus 1 tbsp extra
2 fennel bulbs, quartered and cut into slices 1cm/½in thick
3 portobello mushrooms, about 225g/8oz, cut into slices 1cm/½in thick
3 medium tomatoes, each cut into 6 wedges
vermicelli noodles, to serve (optional)

FOR THE STOCK

1 stalk of lemongrass, white part only, bruised and thinly sliced
1 medium white onion, thinly sliced
3 garlic cloves, sliced
2.5cm/1in ginger, julienned
5cm/2in galangal, julienned

FOR THE GARNISH

a bunch of fresh coriander, leaves picked
4 kaffir lime leaves, ribs removed and thinly sliced

In a large saucepan, put all the stock ingredients, together with 800ml/28fl oz/3¼ cups of water. Bring to the boil, then reduce the heat to low and simmer, uncovered, for 8 minutes. Using a slotted spoon, transfer the stock flavouring ingredients into a small bowl for use later.

Next, stir the coconut milk, sugar, salt and the juice of half the lime into the stock. Stir well and turn off the heat. The soup is now ready.

Heat the oil in a frying pan over a medium-high heat, fry the reserved stock flavouring ingredients for 3 minutes and then tip into the soup.

Using the same pan, and over a medium-high heat, add the remaining oil, then cook the fennel in batches for 2 minutes on each side until nicely charred. Transfer to four serving bowls. Repeat the same for the mushrooms, but cook for just 1 minute on each side, and the tomatoes for 2 minutes on each side.

Pour the soup into the bowls, garnish with the coriander, kaffir lime leaves and lime wedges, and serve with the vermicelli noodles, if using.

Rolled Aubergine Thai Red Curry

Aubergine can be tricky to cook as the timings depend on how big or small you cut the pieces and they float once you add the sauce. I like my vegetables to retain their crunch; I don't like aubergine when it is overcooked and has turned mushy, and all you are left with is the shiny, slippery skin. I have found the best way to enjoy aubergine in this recipe is by cooking it separately from the other vegetables, apart from the peas, to make the dish look colourful. There's a bit of work involved with grilling and rolling the aubergine slices, but trust me, you certainly will enjoy the end result.

SERVES 4

3 aubergines, about 250g/9oz each
1 tbsp vegetable oil, plus 2 tbsp extra
20 fresh Thai basil leaves
½ tbsp palm sugar
1 tsp fine sea salt
1 tbsp light soy sauce
2 tbsp frozen peas
200ml/7fl oz/scant 1 cup coconut milk
salt and pepper
jasmine rice, to serve

FOR THE RED CURRY PASTE

3 red chillies, deseeded
1 banana shallot, peeled
1 stalk of lemongrass, trimmed
2.5cm/1in galangal
3 garlic cloves, peeled
1 tsp ground coriander
½ tsp ground cumin
10 sprigs of fresh coriander, including stalks
1 tbsp tamarind paste

Blitz together the paste ingredients with 2 tablespoons of water using a handheld stick blender until fine and smooth. Set aside.

Cut the stalks off the aubergines and cut lengthways into 1cm/½in slices. Brush the aubergine with oil on both sides and season with salt and pepper.

Heat a griddle or frying pan over a medium-high heat. Add the aubergine and cook in batches for 1 minute on each side. If the pan is looking dry, add more oil.

Remove from the pan, place on a chopping board, wait for 2–3 minutes to cool and then roll each slice from the wide end to the top and arrange in the centre of a large serving dish. Cover with aluminium foil to keep warm and set aside.

Heat the remaining 2 tablespoons of oil in a medium saucepan over a medium-low heat. Fry the Thai basil for 1 minute until crispy. Remove from the pan with a slotted spoon and drain on kitchen paper to remove any excess oil.

Using the oil left in the pan, increase the heat to medium, stir in the paste and cook for 3 minutes. Next, add the sugar, salt and soy sauce and continue to cook for 2 minutes. Add the peas, cook for a further minute and then stir in the coconut milk, together with 100ml/3½fl oz/scant ½ cup of water. Bring to the boil and reduce the heat to low. Simmer for 3 minutes. Turn off the heat and gently pour the sauce over the aubergine in the bowl. Just before serving, garnish with the Thai basil and serve with jasmine rice.

Sweet Potato, Tomato & Spinach Curry

To achieve a good curry, the paste must be fried lightly with oil to begin with so that the moisture in the paste evaporates, and the paste becomes even more fragrant and delicious. This method is known as *tumis* in Malay, and the paste is ready when the oil has split. As I have reduced the amount of oil in my recipes, cooking the paste over a low heat for 2–3 minutes is about right, so that the paste cooks gradually and dries up nicely. For this recipe, I cook the sweet potato at the beginning as I like to seal the pieces and give them a slight crispiness, instead of the usual Asian method of simmering in sauce, which can make the potato mushy.

SERVES 4

1 tbsp vegetable oil
600g/1lb 5oz sweet potatoes, peeled and cut into 3cm/1¼in cubes
1 tbsp tamarind paste
1 tsp fine sea salt
½ tbsp palm sugar
1 tbsp light soy sauce
200ml/7fl oz/scant 1 cup coconut milk
2 medium tomatoes, each cut into 8
100g/3½oz baby spinach
4 sprigs of fresh coriander, leaves picked
50g/1¾oz/½ cup roasted cashew nuts, lightly crushed
jasmine rice, to serve

FOR THE PASTE

1 banana shallot, peeled
3 garlic cloves, peeled
3 red chillies, deseeded
1 stalk of lemongrass, trimmed
2.5cm/1in galangal, or ginger with 1 tsp lemon juice
4 kaffir limes leaves, ribs removed
10 sprigs of fresh coriander
1 tbsp ground cumin
½ tbsp ground black pepper
2 green cardamom pods
½ tsp ground nutmeg

Blitz together the paste ingredients with 2 tablespoons of water using a handheld stick blender or food processor until fine and smooth.

Heat the oil in a large saucepan over a medium-high heat and cook the sweet potatoes for 5 minutes, stirring every minute. Reduce the heat to medium-low, stir in the paste and continue to cook for 2 minutes.

Next, add the tamarind, salt, sugar and soy sauce and cook for 1 minute. Stir in the coconut milk, together with 300ml/10fl oz/1¼ cups of water, bring to the boil, then reduce the heat to low and simmer for 6 minutes.

Next, add the tomatoes and spinach and cook for 2 minutes until wilted. Turn off the heat and transfer to a serving bowl. Garnish with coriander and cashew nuts. Serve with jasmine rice.

Cauliflower & Broccoli Curry

Buying mixed ready-chopped cauliflower and broccoli in a bag saves time when preparing this vegan dish. I seasoned the florets with paprika and turmeric to add a bit of flavour.

SERVES 4

200g/7oz cauliflower florets
200g/7oz broccoli florets
1 tsp ground paprika
1 tsp ground turmeric
1 tsp fine sea salt
1 tbsp vegetable oil, plus 2 tbsp extra
1 banana shallot, thinly sliced
2 garlic cloves, thinly sliced
2 tbsp shop-bought Madras curry powder
½ tsp white sugar
1 tbsp tamarind paste
1 x 200g/7oz can chickpeas, rinsed and drained
a handful of fresh parsley, roughly chopped
rice, to serve

In a large bowl, toss together the cauliflower, broccoli, paprika, turmeric and ½ teaspoon of salt until nicely coated.

Heat 1 tablespoon of the oil in a large frying pan over a medium heat. Fry the vegetable mixture for 3 minutes until nicely charred. Transfer to a bowl and set aside.

Using the same pan, heat the remaining oil and sauté the shallot and garlic until golden brown. Add the curry powder, the remaining salt, the sugar and tamarind, stir well and then add 200ml/7fl oz/scant 1 cup of water. Bring to the boil, add the chickpeas and cook for 1 minute.

Next, add the charred cauliflower and broccoli and continue to cook for a further 2 minutes. Turn off the heat and transfer to four serving bowls, garnish with the parsley and serve with rice.

Vegetable Tom Yum

What I love about this soup is that you can be creative with the different sorts of vegetables you can put in it. One of the most common is mushrooms, and here I use fresh shiitake mushrooms for their strong, earthy flavour. This soup is usually served as a side, but I have made it a main by adding Chinese cabbage, cut into strips like flat noodles. You can also include some vermicelli noodles, if you prefer. I made the soup less spicy by not using fiery bird's eye chillies, but if you like your tom yum hot as it is in Thailand, bruise about 4 chillies and add them to the soup when it starts to simmer.

SERVES 4

1 tbsp vegetable oil
1 tbsp palm sugar
2 tsp fine sea salt
3 tbsp tamarind paste
1 tbsp light soy sauce
100g/3½oz fresh shiitake mushrooms, sliced
100g/3½oz fine beans, both ends trimmed, cut into pieces 3cm/1¼in long
1 carrot, about 100g/3½oz, thinly sliced
12 cherry tomatoes, halved
300g/10½oz Chinese cabbage, cut lengthways into 1cm/½in strips
5 kaffir lime leaves, ribs removed and thinly sliced
a handful of fresh coriander, leaves picked

FOR THE PASTE

1 medium white onion, thinly sliced
3 garlic cloves, sliced
3 red chillies, deseeded
2 stalks of lemongrass, white part only, bruised and thinly sliced
5cm/2in galangal

Blitz together the paste ingredients with 2 tablespoons of water using a handheld stick blender or food processor until fine and smooth.

Heat the oil in a large saucepan over a medium-high heat and fry the paste for 3 minutes. Stir in the sugar, salt, tamarind and soy sauce and cook for 1 minute.

Add the mushrooms, beans and carrot, stir well and then pour in 1 litre/36fl oz/4 cups of water. Bring to the boil, then reduce the heat to low and simmer for 10 minutes.

Add the tomatoes, cabbage and kaffir lime leaves and cook for 2 minutes. Turn off the heat, transfer to four serving bowls and garnish with the coriander. Serve immediately.

Lontong

My sister Melissa who lives in The Hague loves to cook this dish with prawns for a family gathering. Usually, it is served during the Eid celebration in Malaysia. There are plenty of condiments to go with the dish, and my simple vegetarian version uses tempeh, tofu, vegetables, boiled eggs and glass noodles.

SERVES 4

1 tbsp vegetable oil
1 tsp fine sea salt
1 tsp palm sugar
1 medium carrot, cut into 4cm/1½in wedges
100g/3½oz fine beans, cut into pieces 4cm/1½in long
300ml/10fl oz/1¼ cups coconut milk
200g/7oz firm tofu, drained and cut into 3cm/1¼in cubes
200g/7oz tempeh, cut into 3cm/1¼in cubes
100g/3½oz glass noodles, soaked in lukewarm water for 15 minutes, then drained
4 eggs, boiled for 8 minutes, peeled and halved
8 sprigs of fresh coriander, leaves picked
1 tbsp shop-bought crispy fried shallots
2 tbsp shop-bought chilli oil

FOR THE PASTE

1 banana shallot, peeled
3 garlic cloves, peeled
2 stalks of lemongrass, trimmed
5cm/2in galangal
5cm/2in fresh turmeric, peeled or 1 tsp ground turmeric

Blitz together the paste ingredients with 2 tablespoons of water using a handheld stick blender or food processor until fine and smooth.

Heat the oil in a large saucepan over a medium-high heat and cook the paste for 3 minutes. Next, add the salt and sugar, stir well, then add the carrot and beans and cook for 1 minute.

Stir in the coconut milk, tofu and tempeh, together with 300ml/10fl oz/1¼ cups of water, bring to the boil, then reduce the heat to low and continue to cook for 5 minutes.

Divide the glass noodles between four serving bowls and ladle some of the sauce with each of the ingredients into each bowl. Place the eggs on top, garnish with the coriander and crispy fried shallots and sprinkle with the chilli oil. Serve immediately.

Vegetarian Banh Mi

I first tried a Vietnamese *banh mi* baguette sandwich in Paris without knowing the true story of how the French baguette became a popular street food in Vietnam, and the way in which the history of colonization has influenced local dishes in many Southeast Asian countries, apart from Thailand which has never been colonized. This baguette is usually served with meat or pâté and pickled vegetables, with spicy sauce. My version is with a mixture of freshly made mushroom pâté with fresh and pickled vegetables. *Banh mi*, which translates literally as 'a baked food containing wheat', makes a perfect picnic dish.

SERVES 4

2 tbsp palm sugar
1 medium carrot, julienned
100g/3½oz white daikon, julienned
4 tbsp rice vinegar
500g/1lb 2oz firm tofu, drained and cut into 4 pieces 1cm/½in thick
½ tbsp vegetable oil
½ tsp ground paprika
2 medium French baguettes
1 Romano red pepper, deseeded and thinly sliced
1 cucumber, cut diagonally into slices 5mm/¼in thick
10 sprigs of fresh coriander, leaves picked
16 fresh mint leaves

FOR THE PÂTÉ

1 tbsp butter
1 banana shallot, finely chopped
100g/3½oz fresh shiitake mushrooms, roughly chopped
100g/3½oz/½ cup quark
salt and pepper

To make the pâté, melt the butter in a large frying pan over a medium heat, sauté the shallot for 2 minutes and then stir in the mushrooms. Season with salt and pepper and cook for 5 minutes until fully softened. Transfer to a food processor, add the quark and blend until fine and smooth. Spoon into a small bowl and chill in the refrigerator for 30 minutes.

Meanwhile, in a medium saucepan, bring 100ml/3½fl oz/scant ½ cup of water to the boil, stir in the sugar and cook for 2 minutes until the sugar is dissolved. Add the carrot and daikon and continue to cook for 30 seconds. Turn off the heat and stir in the vinegar. Set aside for 15 minutes.

For the tofu, brush each slice of tofu with oil, season generously with salt, pepper and the paprika. Place a griddle pan over a high heat and sear the tofu in batches for 2 minutes on each side.

On a board, split the baguettes and use a teaspoon to remove some of the insides to allow room for the filling. To assemble the *banh mi*, spread some pâté on the inside of one half of one baguette, then place some pepper, cucumber, tofu, coriander and mint on top with some drained pickles. Close the baguette, hold firmly and cut into 4 pieces, then transfer 2 pieces into each serving bowl. Repeat for the remaining baguette and serve at once.

Garlic & Pepper Pak Choi, Mushroom & Spinach Stir-fry

Nowadays on weeknights I tend to eat vegetables, while at weekends I will have a selection of meat, fish or seafood. This is something that I picked up during my work as a chef for a Formula One team – seeing how the drivers keep to a very strict but healthy diet monitored by their personal trainers. In Southeast Asia, vegetables are more of a side dish, and in my family, for example, my late mum never failed to include a vegetable side dish for lunch or dinner. She would either cook a single vegetable or a combination, depending on what caught her eye at the local market. For this recipe, I combined pak choi, mushrooms and spinach, and instead of using a ready-made sauce like oyster or mushroom, I made a paste with garlic, ginger, black pepper, soy sauce and sesame oil.

Use long-stemmed spinach for this recipe.

SERVES 4

½ tbsp vegetable oil, plus 1 tbsp extra
250g/9oz button mushrooms, sliced in half
200g/7oz firm tofu, drained and cut into 2cm/¾in cubes
3 pak choi, about 500g/1lb 2oz in total, stems trimmed and leaves cut in half
300g/10½oz long-stemmed spinach, leaves cut in half
2 tbsp sweet soy sauce
½ tbsp black peppercorns, coarsely crushed
2 tbsp sweet soy sauce
6 garlic cloves, finely chopped
1 tsp sesame oil
egg noodles, to serve

Heat ½ tablespoon of the vegetable oil in a wok or large frying pan over a high heat, stir in the mushrooms and tofu and cook for 2 minutes. Add the greens and cook, covered, for 2 minutes.

Open the lid, add the soy sauce and black pepper, stir, and then replace the lid for a further 2 minutes. Transfer to a serving dish and cover with aluminium foil to keep warm.

Wipe the wok or frying pan clean with kitchen paper, heat the remaining 1 tablespoon of vegetable oil over a high heat and fry the garlic for a minute or until golden brown. Turn off the heat and pour the garlic over the vegetables (remove the cover first) followed by the sesame oil. Serve with egg noodles.

Spicy Aubergine & Tempeh Stir-fry

This dish is usually cooked with fiery sambal paste, but for my mild sambal I blended chillies and tomatoes. A traditional food from Java made from fermented soya beans, tempeh is a good complement for the aubergine – the soft aubergine works well with the chunky, nutty texture of the tempeh. This is a good option for anyone looking for something healthy, as tempeh contains no cholesterol and it is a great ingredient for stir-fries and curries.

SERVES 4

2 tbsp vegetable oil
2 tsp palm sugar
1 tsp fine sea salt
1 tbsp tamarind paste
1 aubergine, about 300g/10½oz, cut into slices 1cm/½in thick
400g/14oz tempeh, cut into slices 1cm/½in thick
salt and pepper
jasmine rice, to serve

FOR THE PASTE

1 banana shallot, peeled
3 garlic cloves, peeled
4 red chillies, deseeded
4 medium tomatoes, deseeded
1 stalk of lemongrass, trimmed
1 tbsp light soy sauce

Blitz together the paste ingredients using a handheld stick blender or food processor until fine and smooth.

To make the sambal, heat the oil in a small frying pan over a medium-high heat and cook the paste for 3 minutes. Add the sugar, salt and tamarind and cook for 2 more minutes. Transfer to a large serving bowl.

Heat a griddle pan or heavy-based frying pan over a high heat and cook the aubergine and tempeh in batches for 1½ minutes on each side; season with salt and pepper.

Transfer to the serving bowl on top of the cooked sambal, with the tempeh on one side and the aubergine on the other.

Stir well to coat the aubergine and tempeh evenly with the sambal, then serve immediately with jasmine rice.

Bean & Potato Curry

It is quite rare for me to cook with beans, especially in savoury dishes; in Malaysian cooking, beans are often used in desserts. Using the right blend of spices, these beans tasted really good and I am very pleased with this recipe.

I used ready-cooked beans for this curry as I wanted to make things simple. You can use any type of beans you like, and that includes other vegetables, such as peas, carrots or fine beans. Butternut squash or pumpkin would also make a great replacement for the potatoes, but I recommend you pre-boil them.

SERVES 2–3

2 tbsp vegetable oil
½ tsp cumin seeds
½ tsp black or brown mustard seeds
3 bay leaves
5cm/2in cinnamon stick
1 star anise
1 banana shallot, thinly sliced
2 garlic cloves, finely chopped
2.5cm/1in ginger, finely chopped
2 tbsp shop-bought mild curry powder
1 tbsp tamarind paste
1 tsp fine sea salt
½ tsp white sugar
300g/10½oz baby potatoes, pre-boiled
100ml/3½fl oz/scant ½ cup coconut milk
1 x 200g/7oz can red kidney beans, rinsed and drained
1 x 200g/7oz can edamame, rinsed and drained
1 x 200g/7oz can black beans, rinsed and drained
rice, to serve

Heat the oil in a medium saucepan over a medium heat.

Add the cumin seeds, mustard seeds, bay leaves, cinnamon and star anise. Cook for 1 minute or until fragrant. Next, add the shallot, garlic and ginger. Cook for 2–3 minutes until golden brown.

Stir in the curry powder, together with 300ml/10fl oz/1¼ cups of water. Add the tamarind, salt and sugar. Cook for 3 minutes over a low heat.

Add the potatoes and coconut milk and cook for 2 minutes. Stir in all the beans and cook for 2 minutes, stirring once or twice. Turn off the heat and serve with rice.

Meat & Seafood

les &

Prawn Noodle Soup

Cooking prawns with the heads and shells on adds to the flavour of a dish. This type of noodle soup is famous in Southeast Asia, mainly as an afternoon snack between lunch and dinner. It is served in a large ceramic bowl, and is eaten with chopsticks and a spoon with chilli oil on the side. The broth stays cooking over a low heat all day to keep it warm. It is my favourite dish to cook when it is cold outside and I am craving a hot bowl of soup to help me warm up. I always have a batch of large frozen prawns in my freezer so that I have something easy to cook, and for this simple noodle dish I use ready-made chicken stock. Alternatively, you can use shelled and deveined prawns and add some shop-bought fish balls.

SERVES 2

100g/3½oz fine egg noodles
4 large raw king prawns, heads and shells on
½ tbsp vegetable oil
5cm/2in cinnamon stick
1 star anise
1 medium onion, halved and sliced
3 garlic cloves, sliced
700ml/24fl oz/2¾ cups chicken stock
100g/3½oz bean sprouts
50g/1¾oz baby spinach

FOR THE SEASONING

½ tbsp chilli paste (I recommend sambal badjak)
1 tbsp light soy sauce
1 tbsp fish sauce
1 tsp palm sugar
½ tsp ground white pepper

FOR THE GARNISH

1 spring onion, cut into thin strips and soaked in cold water until curled, then drained
½ red chilli, thinly sliced diagonally
1 tbsp chilli oil (optional)

Cook the egg noodles in a pan of boiling water according to the instructions on the packet. Drain and divide between two serving bowls.

Place the prawns on a chopping board and, using a small, sharp knife, cut along the back of each prawn to remove the vein; this will also help the flesh of the prawn to absorb the flavours of the seasoning. Trim the legs and keep the whiskers for presentation.

Heat the oil in a medium saucepan over a medium-high heat, fry the cinnamon and star anise for 30 seconds, then stir in the onion and garlic and cook for 1 minute.

Add the seasoning ingredients, stir well and then add the prawns. Cook for 1 minute, then stir in the stock. Bring to the boil, and once the prawns have turned pink and curled up nicely, remove with a slotted spoon and transfer to the bowls with the noodles.

Continue to boil the broth over a low heat for 2 minutes and then turn off the heat. Pour the broth into the bowls, add the bean sprouts and spinach, then garnish with the spring onion, chilli and chilli oil, if using. Serve at once.

Minced Beef Noodle Soup

The dark soup for this noodle dish is made using soy and oyster sauces, together with black pepper, which provides a light taste with a tingle of heat. One of the best regional black peppers I have ever used in my cooking was from Sarawak, a Malaysian state on the island of Borneo. The pepper is widely used in local cuisine; it was first grown in 1856 and commercial production began in the early 20th century. It is definitely something to look out for if you are visiting, as I always do, whenever I have the opportunity to visit.

SERVES 2

100g/3½oz fine egg noodles
1 tbsp vegetable oil
5 garlic cloves, finely chopped
200g/7oz minced beef
1 tsp fine sea salt
2 tsp black peppercorns, crushed
600ml/20fl oz/2½ cups beef stock
1 pak choi, quartered
100g/3½oz bean sprouts
1 spring onion, cut into thin strips and soaked in cold water until curled, then drained
½ lime, cut into wedges
1 tbsp shop-bought crispy fried shallots

FOR THE SEASONING

2 tbsp sweet soy sauce
2 tbsp dark soy sauce
2 tbsp oyster sauce
2 tbsp fish sauce

Cook the egg noodles in a pan of boiling water according to the instructions on the packet; drain and set aside.

Mix all the seasoning ingredients together well in a small bowl.

In a medium saucepan, heat the oil over a medium heat and fry the garlic for 1 minute or until fragrant and golden brown, then remove with a slotted spoon and transfer to a small bowl for the garnish.

Using the remaining oil in the pan over a medium heat, add the minced beef, salt and pepper and continue to cook for 2 minutes.

Next, add the stock, together with the seasoning mixture, bring to the boil, then reduce the heat to low and simmer for 3 minutes.

Add the pak choi and cook for 1 minute until wilted, then add the noodles and bean sprouts, cook for 30 seconds and turn off the heat.

Transfer to two serving bowls and top with the spring onion, lime and crispy fried shallots, together with the fried garlic. Serve immediately.

Wok-fried Singapore Noodles with Prawns

One of many things I admire about the Singaporeans is that they are great at promoting their dishes around the world. The food has many great similarities to Malaysian dishes and this causes the occasional dispute over which country a particular dish originates from. I was once interviewed by the *South China Morning Post* about the origin of Hainanese Chicken Rice (see my simple version on page 146). As we already know, the dish originates from southern China, and the same is true of this noodle dish that was actually created in Hong Kong. I absolutely love this dish and highly recommend using Madras curry powder to give the noodles that strongly spiced flavour.

SERVES 4

200g/7oz vermicelli rice noodles
1 tbsp vegetable oil
1 medium onion, halved and thinly sliced
3 garlic cloves, thinly sliced
1 carrot, cut lengthways and sliced diagonally
125g/4½oz mangetout, both ends trimmed
20 raw king prawns, shelled and deveined, but tails left on
200g/7oz bean sprouts
1 spring onion, cut into thin strips and soaked in cold water until curled, the drained
1 red chilli, deseeded and thinly sliced
2 tbsp shop-bought crispy fried shallots (optional)

FOR THE SEASONING

1½ tbsp Madras curry powder
1 tsp ground turmeric
1 tsp fine sea salt
2 tsp white sugar
3 tbsp light soy sauce

Prepare the noodles according to the packet instructions; drain and set aside.

In a small bowl, mix the seasoning ingredients with 2 tablespoons of water and stir well.

Heat the oil in a wok or large frying pan over a medium-high heat. Stir in the onion and garlic and cook for 1 minute. Add the carrot and mangetout, and continue to cook for 2 minutes. Add the prawns and seasoning mixture, cook for 1 minute, then add the noodles and cook for 2 minutes. Next, add the bean sprouts and cook for 1 minute.

Turn off the heat, divide the noodle mixture between four serving bowls and garnish with the spring onion, chilli and crispy fried shallots, if using.

Chicken Noodle Soup

The selection of spices in the soup for this dish makes it aromatic, and the fresh herbs added as the garnish make it fragrant. It is a cross between Vietnamese *pho* and Malaysian *bihun sup*. If you like, use chicken on the bone as this gives the dish more flavour; just simmer for 20 minutes longer over a low heat. Instead of vermicelli noodles, you can use egg or flat rice noodles.

SERVES 2

800ml/28fl oz chicken stock/3¼ cups
300g/10½oz chicken breast fillets, cut into large pieces
1 tbsp light soy sauce
1 tbsp fish sauce
30g/1oz ginger, julienned
½ red onion, thinly sliced, plus ½ extra, thinly sliced, for the garnish
75g/2¾oz vermicelli noodles
150g/5½oz oyster mushrooms, halved
100g/3½oz Chinese broccoli

FOR THE SPICES

5cm/2in cinnamon stick
2 star anise
4 cloves
4 green cardamom pods, lightly bruised
1 tsp coarsely ground black pepper

FOR THE GARNISH

10 fresh mint leaves
10 fresh Thai basil leaves
6 sprigs of fresh coriander, leaves picked
1 red chilli, thinly sliced diagonally
75g/2¾oz bean sprouts

Pour the stock into a large saucepan and add the chicken, soy sauce, fish sauce, ginger, onion and spices. Bring to the boil, then reduce the heat to low and simmer for 10 minutes. Meanwhile, plunge the noodles into a separate pan of boiling water and cook for 4 minutes, then drain. Rinse under cold running water and drain again. Divide between two serving bowls.

After 10 minutes, add the mushrooms and Chinese broccoli to the pan containing the chicken and cook for 2 minutes until softened.

Using tongs, remove the chicken pieces and place on a chopping board. Shred into thin strips using a couple of forks. Put the shredded chicken on top of the noodles in the serving bowls.

Lift the vegetables from the pan using the tongs and put on top of the noodles, next to the chicken.

Ladle the soup into the bowls and then add the garnish ingredients next to the chicken and vegetables. Serve immediately.

Spicy Beef Noodle Soup

It is common for Asian soups to be spiced up using bird's eye chillies, and I have to say that most Asian chefs are not shy when it comes to using them. I have learned to appreciate that not all dishes have to be spicy and, if a dish is too hot, it is not possible to taste any flavour other than chilli. This is something I have tried to explain to my chilli-loving friends, but their taste buds are so used to having chilli in everything they eat, without it there is no kick. For this dish, I recommend using just 4 chillies, but you can leave them out completely if your tolerance for heat is lower than mine.

SERVES 4

- 250g/9oz vermicelli noodles
- 400g/14oz beef (in one piece), chuck steak is recommended
- 10 sprigs of fresh coriander, leaves picked
- 150g/5½oz bean sprouts
- 1 red chilli, thinly sliced diagonally
- 1 lime, cut into wedges (optional)
- 2 tbsp shop-bought crispy fried shallots

FOR THE SOUP

- 1.5 litres/54fl oz/xx cups beef stock
- 1 stalk of lemongrass, thinly sliced diagonally
- 4 bird's eye chillies, bruised
- 1 medium onion, thinly sliced
- 2 tbsp chilli paste (I recommend sambal badjak)
- 2 tbsp fish sauce
- 2 tsp palm sugar
- 4 kaffir lime leaves, bruised

In a heatproof bowl, cover the noodles with boiling water, leave to soak for 4 minutes, then drain and rinse with cold water until completely cool to stop the noodles continuing to cook and becoming too soft. Set aside.

Put all the soup ingredients into a large saucepan, add the beef, bring to the boil, then reduce the heat, partly cover and simmer for 30 minutes, or until the beef is tender.

Remove the piece of beef to a chopping board and slice very thinly with a sharp knife.

Divide the noodles between four serving bowls, lay the beef slices on top, ladle the soup over the beef and noodles and then garnish with the coriander, bean sprouts, chilli, lime, if using, and the crispy fried shallots. Serve immediately.

Chicken Curry Noodles

Malaysia is known for the diversity of its people and its food. This dish is elaborate and includes a large number of ingredients to give a rich flavour. If you can source Malaysian curry powder, use 2 tablespoons of that instead of the ground mixed spices listed below; you can also use Madras curry powder.

SERVES 4

100g/3½oz fine beans, both ends trimmed and cut into 1cm/½in pieces
150g/5½oz bean sprouts
300g/10½oz fine egg noodles
2 tbsp vegetable oil
1 cinnamon stick
1 star anise
3 bay leaves (or a sprig of curry leaves)
3 tbsp chilli paste (I recommend sambal badjak)
2 tsp fine sea salt
1 tsp white sugar
1 tbsp tamarind paste
500g/1lb 2oz boneless chicken thighs, cut into thin strips
200ml/7fl oz/scant 1 cup coconut milk
1.2 litres/42fl oz/5 cups chicken stock

FOR THE PASTE

2 banana shallots, peeled
5 garliccloves, peeled
2.5cm/1in ginger
2 stalks of lemongrass, trimmed

FOR THE GROUND MIXED SPICES

2 tbsp ground coriander
½ tbsp ground cumin
½ tbsp ground fennel
1 tsp ground turmeric

FOR THE GARNISH

4 eggs, boiled for 8 minutes, peeled and halved
8 sprigs of fresh coriander, leaves picked
1 red chilli, thinly sliced
1 lime, cut into 4 wedges

Blitz together the paste ingredients using a handheld stick blender or food processor. Add 2 tbsp of water until fine and smooth.

In a small bowl, mix the ground spices with 100ml/3½fl oz/scant ½ cup of water.

Put the beans into a bowl and add enough boiling water until well covered. Blanch for 1 minute and then spoon out into a bowl. Using the same water, blanch the bean sprouts for 30 seconds and then transfer to the same bowl as the beans.

Using fresh boiling water, repeat the same method for the egg noodles and blanch for 3 minutes. (Please refer to the instructions on the packet if you are using a different size of egg noodles.) Transfer to the bowl with the beans.

Heat a large saucepan over a medium heat. Add the oil, cinnamon, star anise and bay leaves. Once the spices have started to sizzle and release their aroma, add the paste and sauté for 2 minutes until fragrant.

Next, add the chilli paste and spice mixture. Cook for 1 minute, then add the salt, sugar and tamarind and cook for a further minute. Add the chicken and cook for 3 minutes to seal the meat.

Stir in the coconut milk and cook for 1 minute. Stir in the chicken stock and bring to the boil, then reduce the heat to low. Simmer for 5 minutes, stirring once or twice.

To serve, divide the beans, bean sprouts and noodles between four serving bowls, and pour over the chicken curry. Garnish with the eggs, coriander, chilli and lime wedges.

Spicy Beef Noodle Soup p.138

Chicken Curry Noodles p. 139

Prawn Pad Thai

When anyone asks about the best Thai dishes that have been exported around the world, Pad Thai is certainly among the most sought after. My visit to the country's capital in search of the best Pad Thai in Bangkok revealed how easy it actually is to cook this dish. It has a wonderful combination of sweet, sour and salty flavours with a good crunch of peanuts. Forget about ready-made sauce in a jar, you can make your own by combining tamarind, palm sugar, fish sauce and soy sauce – it's as simple as that.

SERVES 2

200g/7oz flat rice noodles
½ tbsp vegetable oil, plus extra for the egg
3 garlic cloves, finely chopped
10 raw king prawns, shelled and deveined, but tails left on
1 egg
125g/4½oz bean sprouts
50g/1¾oz garlic chives (kow choi)

FOR THE SEASONING

1½ tbsp tamarind paste
1 tbsp palm sugar
1 tbsp fish sauce
2 tbsp light soy sauce

FOR THE GARNISH

1 spring onion, cut into thin strips and soaked in cold water until curled, then drained
10 sprigs of fresh coriander, leaves picked
2 tsp dried chilli flakes
½ lime, cut into 2 wedges
2 tbsp salted peanuts, lightly crushed

Prepare the noodles according to the packet instructions; drain and set aside.

In a small bowl, mix the seasoning ingredients with 2 tablespoons of water and stir well.

Heat the oil in a wok or large frying pan over a high heat. Fry the garlic for 30 seconds, then add the prawns and cook for 1 minute. Push the prawns to one side of the wok or frying pan and drizzle in a little more oil. Crack in the egg, scramble it, cook until dry and then add the noodles and seasoning mixture. Cook for 2 minutes, then stir in the bean sprouts and chives, continue to cook for 1 more minute and then turn off the heat.

Transfer to two serving bowls and garnish with the spring onion, coriander, chilli flakes, lime wedges and peanuts. Serve at once.

Noodles with Squid

Scoring squid requires a bit of skill and practice: start by running the knife slowly over the squid; once you are more confident, you will be able to score it faster. Scoring makes the squid look attractive and also allows the flavours to coat the surface and penetrate the flesh. I keep having to remind students in the masterclasses that I run regularly in the UK and Europe to score inside of the tube and not the outside. I threaten them by saying that I will check all of their pans to see if this has been done correctly – of course, I am joking, but I like my classes to have a fun element.

SERVES 2

125g/4½oz vermicelli noodles
2 squid tubes, about 125g/4½oz each, cleaned
½ tbsp vegetable oil
3 garlic cloves, thinly sliced
1 tbsp light soy sauce, plus 1 tbsp extra
75g/2¾oz baby spinach
2 tbsp oyster sauce
1 tsp ground white pepper
100g/3½oz bean sprouts
1 spring onion, cut into thin strips and soaked in cold water until curled, then drained
1 tbsp shop-bought crispy fried shallots
1 red chilli, thinly sliced diagonally (optional)

Prepare the noodles according to the packet instructions, then drain and set aside.

Place the squid on a chopping board and cut through both sides to open them out flat.

Using a sharp knife, score shallow diagonal cuts in a criss-cross pattern on the inside surface. Be very gentle to avoid cutting all the way through the squid.

Heat the oil in a wok or large frying pan over a high heat and fry the garlic for 30 seconds until fragrant and turning golden brown. Add the squid and soy sauce, continue to cook for 30 seconds and then stir in the noodles, spinach, oyster sauce, white pepper and the remaining soy sauce. Cook for 2 minutes, add the bean sprouts and continue to cook for 1 minute.

Turn off the heat and transfer to two serving bowls. Garnish with the spring onion, crispy fried shallots and chilli, if using, and serve.

Curried Chicken Rice

I cooked this dish many times before and during my student years in the 1990s. I graduated from the University of Portsmouth with a degree in Construction Management and I never thought that one day I would become a full-time chef. It was all due to my passion for cooking. My student friends knew that if they visited my place they would always be served this rice – it was cheap and easy to cook. I marinated the chicken with the spices and seasoning the night before to allow the meat to absorb the flavours of the spices. Here I made my own ground mixed spices, but if you can buy a packet of Malaysian curry powder, use 3 tablespoons of that, or you can just use Madras curry powder.

SERVES 4

600g/1lb 5oz boneless chicken thighs, cut into bite-sized pieces
2 tbsp vegetable oil
5cm/2in cinnamon stick
1 star anise
3 bay leaves
1 banana shallot, sliced
3 garlic cloves, sliced
2.5cm/1in ginger, finely chopped
400g/14oz/2 cups basmati rice, rinsed
800ml/28fl oz/3¼ cups chicken stock
4 tbsp frozen peas
a handful of fresh mint leaves
a handful of fresh coriander, leaves picked

FOR THE GROUND MIXED SPICES

1½ tbsp ground coriander
2 tsp ground cumin
1 tsp ground fennel
2 tsp mild chilli powder
1 tsp ground turmeric

Combine the ground mixed spices, salt, sugar and coconut milk in a mixing bowl, then add the chicken pieces and stir to coat. Marinate the chicken for 30 minutes or preferably overnight in the fridge.

Heat the oil in a large saucepan over a medium-high heat, add the cinnamon, star anise and bay leaves and cook for 30 seconds to infuse the oil.

Stir in the shallot, garlic and ginger and cook for 2 minutes until fragrant. Add the chicken, together with the marinade, and cook for 5 minutes.

Add the rice and stir well, then pour over the stock and stir again. Bring to the boil and continue to cook for 4 minutes, then reduce the heat to low, add the peas and cook for 10 minutes.

Cover the pan with aluminium foil and allow to rest for 5 minutes with the heat turned off. Divide the rice mixture between four serving bowls and garnish with the mint and coriander leaves. Serve immediately.

One Pot Chicken Rice

I adapted this recipe from the famous dish known as Hainanese chicken rice, which was introduced to many countries in Southeast Asia by immigrants from Hainan province in southern China, especially Malaysia and Singapore. The rice is infused with ginger and sesame oil, cooked with chicken stock and served with soy sauce, chilli dressing and vegetables on the side. I added ground turmeric to give the rice a vivid yellow colour.

SERVES 4

1 tbsp vegetable oil
5 garlic cloves, sliced
50g/1¾oz ginger, thinly sliced
1 spring onion, split lengthways
4 chicken thigh fillets on the bone, about 600g/1lb 5oz in total
4 tbsp light soy sauce
700ml/24fl oz/2¾ cups chicken stock
400g/14oz/2 cups long grain rice, washed
1 tsp ground white pepper
½ tsp ground turmeric
1 tsp sesame oil
1 large Little Gem lettuce, leaves picked
1 cucumber, peeled into ribbons and rolled
8 cherry tomatoes, halved

FOR THE SOY SEASONING

4 tbsp light soy sauce
1 tsp sesame oil
2.5cm/1in ginger, finely chopped

FOR THE CHILLI DRESSING

2 red chillies, deseeded
5 garlic cloves, peeled
1 tbsp palm sugar
juice of 1 lime

In a small bowl, mix all the ingredients for the soy seasoning together with 100ml/3½fl oz/ scant ½ cup of water. Set aside.

Blitz together the chilli dressing ingredients with 80ml/2¾fl oz/5½ tbsp of water using a handheld stick blender or food processor until a fine and smooth consistency.

Heat the vegetable oil in a large saucepan over a medium-high heat and fry the garlic, ginger and spring onion for 2 minutes until fragrant.

Add the chicken and soy sauce and cook for 3 minutes to seal the chicken. Pour in the stock and bring to the boil, then continue to cook for 2 minutes.

Add the rice, white pepper and turmeric, stir well and cook for 8 minutes, then reduce the heat to low, cover and cook for 4 minutes.

Turn off the heat, sprinkle over the sesame oil and cover the pan with aluminium foil to trap the steam and let the rice fluff up for 5 minutes. Divide the rice between four serving bowls.

Serve the chicken rice in a large serving bowl and put the lettuce, cucumber and tomatoes next to the rice in the bowl. Serve with the soy sauce seasoning and chilli dressing on the side.

Squid Fried Rice

Nasi goreng, or egg fried rice, is a breakfast dish in Southeast Asia. In the household it is decided the night before what breakfast will be if there is any leftover rice.

In cafés and restaurants, this dish is also served in the evenings and comes with fried egg, crispy chicken and vegetables on the side.

SERVES 2

2 squid tubes, about 125g/4½oz each, cleaned
1 tbsp vegetable oil, plus ½ tbsp extra to fry the egg
3 garlic cloves, thinly sliced
1 medium onion, diced
1 tbsp light soy sauce
1 egg
300g/10½oz/1½ cups white rice, cooked and chilled
½ tbsp chilli paste (I recommend sambal badjak)
1 tbsp sweet soy sauce
1 tbsp frozen peas
4 sprigs of fresh coriander, leaves picked
1 tbsp shop-bought crispy fried shallots
1 chilli, thinly sliced diagonally (optional)

Place the squid tubes on a chopping board, cut through on both sides to open them out flat.

Using a sharp knife, score shallow diagonal cuts in a criss-cross pattern on the inside surface. Be very gentle to avoid cutting all the way through the squid.

Heat the oil in a fry wok or large frying pan over a high heat and fry the garlic and onion for 2 minutes until fragrant and golden brown. Add the squid, together with ½ tablespoon of light soy sauce, and cook for 1 minute until the squid has curled up.

Sprinkle over the remaining oil and crack in the egg, scramble and cook it until set, then add the squid and mix together.

Stir in the rice, chilli paste, sweet soy sauce, peas and the remaining light soy sauce. Cook for 2 minutes, stirring constantly, and then turn off the heat.

Divide the fried rice between two serving bowls and garnish with the coriander, crispy fried shallots and chilli, if using. Serve immediately.

Nood

Vegetarian & Plant-based

Plant-based Noodle Soup

One thing I like about this noodle soup is that it comes with lots of fresh herbs – a combination of fresh coriander, mint and Thai basil. Adapted from Vietnamese *pho*, this dish is my way of cooking with purely plant-based ingredients. The base flavour for the soup comes from the strong, earthy flavour of shiitake mushrooms and is infused with spices and herbs.

SERVES 4

250g/9oz vermicelli noodles
200g/7oz Chinese broccoli, or pak choi cut in half

FOR THE SOUP

12 dried shiitake mushrooms, soaked in boiling water for 15 minutes or until soft, then drained
1 red onion, thinly sliced
50g/1¾oz ginger, julienned
5cm/2in cinnamon stick
2 star anise
4 green cardamom pods, lightly bruised
4 cloves
4 tbsp mushroom stir-fry sauce
2 tsp fine sea salt
1 tbsp freshly ground black pepper
2 tsp palm sugar

FOR THE GARNISH

1 red onion, thinly sliced
150g/5½oz bean sprouts
10 sprigs of fresh coriander, leaves picked
20 fresh Thai basil leaves
20 fresh mint leaves
1 red chilli, thinly sliced diagonally
1 lime, cut into wedges

Soak the noodles in boiling water for 4 minutes, covered. Drain and set aside.

Put all the soup ingredients into a large saucepan with 1.5 litres/54fl oz of water. Bring to the boil, reduce the heat to low and simmer for 10 minutes.

Next, add the Chinese broccoli (or pak choi) and cook for 2 minutes.

Divide the noodles between four deep serving bowls and, using tongs, transfer the broccoli (or pak choi) and mushrooms into the bowls and gently ladle over the soup. Top each bowl with some of the garnish ingredients. Serve at once.

Wok-fried Noodles with Asparagus & Enoki Mushrooms

This is one of my favourite noodle dishes that I love to cook for an easy weeknight dinner. The enoki mushrooms have a mild and fruity flavour compared to other types of mushroom and here provide an alternative to the usual bean sprouts in stir-fried noodles. The best way to store the mushrooms in the fridge is by wrapping them, unwashed, in paper. I only wash them when I am ready to cook with them.

SERVES 2

200g/7oz flat rice noodles, 5mm/¼in wide
1 tbsp vegetable oil
3 garlic cloves, thinly sliced
1 onion, halved and thinly sliced
100g/3½oz asparagus tips
200g/7oz enoki mushrooms

FOR THE SEASONING

2 tbsp sweet soy sauce
3 tbsp light soy sauce
2 tbsp chilli oil with flakes

Plunge the noodles into a pan of boiling water and cook for 8 minutes, or follow the instructions on the packet. Drain thoroughly, rinse with cold water and set aside. This helps to remove the excess starch from the noodles.

In a small bowl, mix all the seasoning ingredients together well.

Heat the oil in a wok or large frying pan over a high heat and stir-fry the garlic and onion for 2 minutes or until golden brown.

Add the asparagus and continue to fry for a further minute, stirring once or twice. Add the noodles, mix well and stir in the seasoning mixture. Cook for 2 minutes, then add the mushrooms and continue to cook for a further minute.

Turn off the heat, transfer to two serving bowls and serve immediately.

Leek & Tomato Noodles

The thick sauce for these noodles is heavily based on tomato and seasoned with soy sauce. I adapted this dish from the Indonesian *mie godog*, which is usually cooked with chicken stock, and for my vegetarian version, I used leek, carrot, cabbage and tomato. The egg is added to thicken up the sauce, but you can exclude it for the vegan option and replace the egg noodles with vermicelli noodles.

SERVES 2

125g/4½oz egg noodles
1 tbsp vegetable oil
1 banana shallot, finely chopped
3 garlic cloves, finely chopped
1 medium leek, cut into slices 5mm/¼in thick
1 carrot, about 100g/3½oz, sliced
1 tomato, deseeded and diced
100g/3½oz white cabbage, thinly sliced
1 egg
½ red chilli, thinly sliced diagonally
4 sprigs of fresh coriander, leaves picked

FOR THE SEASONING

1 tbsp tomato purée
1 tsp coarsely ground black pepper
2 tbsp sweet soy sauce
2 tbsp light soy sauce
1 tsp palm sugar
1 tsp fine sea salt

Plunge the noodles into a pan of boiling water and cook for 8 minutes, or follow the instructions on the packet. Drain the noodles thoroughly, rinse with cold water and set aside. This helps to remove excess starch from the noodles.

In a small bowl, mix all the seasoning ingredients together well.

Heat the oil in a saucepan over a medium heat and fry the shallot and garlic for 2 minutes until golden brown, then stir in the leek, carrot and tomato and continue to cook for 2 minutes.

Next, add the seasoning mixture, stir well and then pour in 300ml/10fl oz/1¼ cups of water. Bring to the boil, then add the noodles and cabbage, stir well and push everything to one side. Crack in the egg and let it cook for 1 minute, then fold it in with all the other ingredients, continue to cook for a further minute and then turn off the heat.

Transfer to two serving bowls and garnish with the chilli and coriander. Serve at once.

Tempeh & Vegetable Wok-fried Noodles with Egg Ribbons

This quick noodle dish is not like a typical wok-fried noodle dish with soy sauce. It has a strong curry flavour from the ground mixed spices – you can use shop-bought spices or make your own using my simple recipe, see below. I added tempeh for this dish, one of my essential frozen ingredients, but you can substitute this with firm tofu if preferred, and use the same frying method as for tempeh below.

Using a wok to cook this dish is highly recommended, but a large frying pan will work too. It is all about creating enough room for the ingredients to be in contact with the wok or the base of the pan over a high heat, and ensuring that all the ingredients are prepared in advance, as cooking this dish is super-fast as it is made on the streets in Southeast Asia; there it is even more of a challenge, as they mostly cook over charcoal that is constantly on a high heat, and this gives a beautiful smoky flavour to the noodles.

SERVES 2–3

150g/5½oz fine or medium egg noodles, or 300g/10½oz straight-to-wok noodles
1 tbsp vegetable oil, plus 1½ tbsp extra for frying the tempeh
1 egg, beaten
100g/3½oz tempeh, cut into 1cm/½in slices
3 garlic cloves, finely chopped
1 banana shallot, peeled
100g/3½oz fine beans, both ends trimmed, then cut into pieces 3cm/1¼in long
2 tbsp light soy sauce
½ tbsp palm sugar
1 tsp fine sea salt
200g/7oz bean sprouts
4 sprigs of fresh coriander, leaves picked

FOR THE GROUND MIXED SPICES

1 tbsp ground coriander
1 tsp ground cumin
2 tsp mild chilli powder
1 tsp ground turmeric

Plunge the noodles into a large pan of boiling water, turn off the heat and blanch for 4 minutes. Drain well, rinse with cold water and toss with ½ tablespoon of oil. Set aside. (You can skip this step if you are using straight-to-wok noodles.)

In a small bowl, mix the ground mixed spices with 100ml/3½fl oz/scant ½ cup of water and stir well.

Heat ½ tablespoon of oil in a wok or large frying pan over a medium heat, carefully add the egg and shake it into an even layer. Cover the wok or pan with a lid and cook for 1 minute or until set. Slip the egg from the wok or pan onto a chopping board and let it cool for 2 minutes. Roll up the egg tightly and cut into pieces 5mm/¼in wide with a sharp knife. Set aside.

Wipe the wok or pan clean with kitchen paper and heat the remaining 1½ tablespoons of oil over a medium-low heat. Fry the tempeh for 2 minutes on each side or until crispy. Remove with a slotted spoon, transfer to a plate and dab with kitchen paper to remove any excess oil.

Using the remaining oil in the wok or pan, increase the heat to medium-high and fry the garlic and shallot for 2 minutes. Stir in the spice mixture, cook for a further minute and then add the beans. Cook for 2 minutes, then add the noodles, soy sauce, sugar and salt, together with 50ml/1¾fl oz/3 tbsp of water, and continue to cook for 2 minutes. Next, stir in the bean sprouts and tempeh and cook for a further minute. Turn off the heat, transfer to serving bowls and garnish with the egg ribbons and coriander. Serve at once.

Lazy Noodles

Just to clarify, the word lazy here refers to me – not the noodles. I am constantly asked about what I eat at home after cooking all day in the kitchen and this dish is the answer. I love noodles, especially egg noodles, but I am not so keen on instant or pot noodles. The latter reminds me of my student years on a tight budget, which I am sure many people can relate to. Fine egg noodles are the best to use for this dish, and if you ever cook it, please tag me on social media so I know that you are enjoying my recommended lazy moment.

SERVES 2

150g/5½oz fine egg noodles
1 pak choi, cut into 2.5cm/1in wide pieces
2 tbsp chilli oil (Lao Gan Ma crispy chilli oil is recommended)
2 tbsp light soy sauce
1 tsp sesame oil
½ tsp ground white pepper

In a large heatproof bowl, pour boiling water over the noodles and pak choi, cover the bowl and let them soften for 8 minutes. Drain in a sieve and put both ingredients back into the bowl.

Add all the other ingredients to the bowl and mix well.

Transfer to two serving bowls and enjoy your lazy moment.

Plant-based Fried Rice

One of the many good habits I picked up after living in the Netherlands for three years, apart from cycling, was eating more vegetarian or vegan dishes on weeknights, and keeping meat or seafood dishes for the weekend. This dish was adapted from my usual cauliflower fried rice recipe. Cauliflower rice that comes in a packet is easy to find in Dutch supermarkets. If you can buy this (or make your own), replace the white rice in the recipe with cauliflower rice, and the cauliflower florets with broccoli.

SERVES 4

1 tbsp vegetable oil
1 medium onion, halved and thinly sliced
200g/7oz cauliflower, cut into small florets
1 leek, cut into 5mm/¼in slices
1 medium carrot, cut in half lengthways, then thinly sliced diagonally
125g/4½oz Chinese broccoli, or pak choi, stems bruised and cut into pieces 3cm/1¼in wide
1 tbsp light soy sauce, plus 2 tbsp extra for the rice
500g/1lb 2oz/xx cups cooked white rice
1 tsp ground white pepper
½ tsp fine sea salt
½ tbsp sesame oil
2 spring onions, cut into thin strips and soaked in cold water until curled, then drained
2 tbsp shop-bought crispy fried shallots

Heat the vegetable oil in a wok or large frying pan over a high heat. Fry the onion for 2 minutes until golden brown.

Add the cauliflower, leek, carrot and Chinese broccoli (or pak choi), together with 1 tablespoon of soy sauce. Stir well, cover and cook for 3 minutes, stirring every minute.

Open the lid and stir in the rice, together with the white pepper, salt, the remaining soy sauce and the sesame oil, and cook for 2 minutes. Turn off the heat and transfer to four serving bowls. Garnish with the spring onions and crispy fried shallots. Serve immediately.

King Mushroom Clay pot Rice

The beauty of cooking rice in a clay pot is that it retains the heat and maintains a steady temperature, allowing the rice to cook perfectly, in the same way as a heavy-based pan. But these days not all modern kitchens have a clay pot as the traditional way is for them to be cooked over a charcoal fire. Clay pots are relatively inexpensive and can be bought in most Chinese supermarkets or online – they can also be put in the oven. You don't have to have a clay pot to cook this dish and here I just used a normal saucepan. I made the king oyster mushrooms look like scallops; they have a nice soft texture that goes well with the flavour of claypot rice.

SERVES 4

- 4 king oyster mushrooms, about 100g/3½oz each, cut into 3cm/1¼in 'scallop-sized' pieces
- 1 medium onion, thinly sliced
- 8 dried shiitake mushrooms, soaked in boiling water for 15 minutes or until soft, then drained
- 2 tsp sesame oil
- 400g/14oz/2 cups long grain rice, rinsed
- 2 pak choi, quartered
- 1 spring onion, cut into thin strips and soaked in cold water until curled, then drained
- salt and pepper

FOR THE SEASONING

- 2 tbsp light soy sauce
- 1 tbsp mushroom stir-fry sauce
- 3 garlic cloves, finely chopped
- 2.5cm/1in ginger, finely chopped

Heat a large, non-stick frying pan over a medium-low heat and cook the king oyster mushrooms in batches for 2 minutes on each side. Season with salt and pepper. Set aside.

Put the onion, shiitake mushrooms and sesame oil in a large, deep saucepan, together with 700ml/24fl oz/2¾ cups of water, bring to the boil, then stir in the rice and reduce the heat to medium-low. Cover the pan with a lid, leaving it slightly open, and continue to cook for 5 minutes.

Next, add the pak choi and the seasoning ingredients, stir well and continue to cook for 3 minutes over a low heat.

Open the lid, add the king oyster mushrooms, cover the pan with aluminium foil to trap the steam, continue to cook over a low heat for 2 minutes and then turn off the heat. Allow to rest for 5 minutes, then divide between four serving bowls and garnish with the spring onion. Serve at once.

Vegetarian Biryani with Chickpeas

I visited Singapore many years ago on holiday and stumbled across a wonderful, well-organized food court whose name I can't recall, but I vividly remember the stall that served delicious biryani. The chef showed me all the layers in the huge cooking pot he used to cook the aromatic rice. This experience always comes to mind every time I cook or read anything about biryani.

SERVES 4

FOR THE JACKFRUIT & CHICKPEA CURRY

2 tbsp ghee, butter or vegan spread, plus ½ tbsp extra for the rice
4 white onions, halved and thinly sliced
4 medium and ripe tomatoes, finely chopped
1 x 565g/20oz can jackfruit in brine, drained and rinsed
1 x 400g/14oz can chickpeas, drained and rinsed

FOR THE RICE

500g/1lb 2oz/2½ cups basmati rice, soaked in water for 20 minutes then drained
3 green cardamom pods, lightly bruised
3 cloves
1 cinnamon stick
10 black peppercorns
1 tsp cumin seeds
2 tsp salt

FOR THE SAUCE

200g/7oz/scant 1 cup quark or natural yogurt
2.5cm/1in ginger, finely chopped
5 garlic cloves, sliced
1 tbsp ground coriander
2 tsp ground cumin
2 tsp mild chilli powder
1 tsp ground turmeric
2 tsp salt
1 tsp garam masala
10 sprigs of fresh coriander, roughly chopped
20 fresh mint leaves, roughly chopped
4 tbsp frozen peas

TO FINISH

3 tsp saffron water (a pinch of saffron threads soaked in 2 tbsp warm water for 20 minutes)
3 tsp rose water
20 fresh mint leaves, roughly chopped
10 sprigs of fresh coriander, roughly chopped

To make the curry, melt the ghee, butter or spread in a large saucepan over a medium-high heat. Next, stir in the onions and fry for 10 minutes until golden to dark brown. Remove half the onion and set aside for later use.

Stir in the tomatoes and cook for 3 minutes until softened. Add the jackfruit, chickpeas and all the sauce ingredients, except for the peas, and cook for 10 minutes. Stir in the peas, together with 200ml/7fl oz/scant 1 cup of water, and cook for a further 2 minutes. Turn off the heat.

Meanwhile, place 1.8 litres/63fl oz/7½ cups of water in a large saucepan and add the spices and salt, then bring to the boil and stir in the rice. Cook for 8 minutes. After the first 4 minutes, reduce the heat to medium-low and continue to cook for the remaining 4 minutes. Turn off the heat and drain.

Put the remaining ghee, butter or spread in a deep saucepan and scatter over one-third of the rice followed by 1 teaspoon of the saffron water and 1 teaspoon of the rose water. Scatter over one-third of the mint, coriander and fried onions, followed by one-third of the curry. Repeat the same process until everything has been used.

Cover the pan with aluminium foil, put over a low heat and cook for 8 minutes. Turn off the heat and let the biryani rest for 5 minutes, then remove the foil and divide between four serving bowls. Serve at once.

About the Author

Born in Penang, Malaysia, Norman moved to the UK in 1994 and studied Construction Management. After graduating and working in the construction industry, he switched his career to become a full-time chef and restauranteur in 2006.

In 2010 Norman joined the Formula One Lotus Team as the race chef, working all over the globe. His travels sparked an ambition to promote Malaysian cuisine around the world. He has appeared on MasterChef Malaysia, Tom Kerridge's 'Best Ever Dishes' on BBC 2 and Channel 4's 'Sunday Brunch' and has featured in numerous magazines in the UK and Malaysia. He has also hosted five seasons of his own cooking show on Malaysian TV.

He received the UK's Young Asian & Oriental Chef of the Year Award in 2012 and in the same year became a member of the Hospitality Guild's Young Hall of Fame. He was appointed as the Kuala Lumpur Food Ambassador in 2015, promoting the gastronomic city to the European market. His first book *Amazing Malaysian* was published in 2016 and translated into Dutch in 2019. He teaches Malaysian and Southeast Asian cookery classes at cookery schools across the UK and Netherlands.

Norman is currently based in Leeds, UK and holds the Executive Chef position at Kuala Lumpur Restaurant & Bar in Horsforth, Leeds as well as Masterclass developer and tutor for the wagamama Chef Academy. He is active on social media and his full profile and achievements are available on www.normanmusa.com.

Acknowledgments

Words cannot describe the joy I felt when my dearest literary agent, Heather Holden-Brown told me I was to write another book. I am taking this opportunity to thank all the amazing people that made this dream happen.

Heather, I don't know how many times I told you this, you are my guardian angel and the best dim sum lunch date ever. Thank you for always believing in me and recognising my hard work and passion.

I was first introduced to Cara Armstrong, the book editor by Heather and simply thrilled to be given this opportunity working together on this book. Thank you so much for always allowing me to be creative and appreciate my passion. You are the best editor anyone could ask for. Thanks also for putting together the perfect dream team to work with. Thanks also to Laura Russell for the work for this book and spending time looking after the dream team during the photoshoot.

Nicole Herft, we met donkey years ago for my first TV debut 'The Market Kitchen' and I always remembered your great energy, personality and amazing food styling skills. Every dish you styled was a perfection. Thank you for sharing your talent in this book. Holly Cochrane, thank you for preparing and cooking my dishes to precision. I could listen to you and Nicole chatting away in the kitchen all day, and felt like I caught all the latest news in the industry. Such fun.

Luke J Albert, thank you for capturing the dishes beautifully with amazing colour and detail. I was in awe of your gadgets as soon I stepped into the studio and knew right away that the photos would look amazing.

The Evi-O.Studio team, we never met, but I am sure we will one day when I travel down under. Thank you so much for designing this book beautifully, those eye catching patterned bowls are simply iconic.

To my sister Melissa Menist in The Netherlands, thank you for sharing some fun times cooking in the kitchen and looking after me all the time. You gave me the family love that I have yearned for since losing my parents. Every human walks around with a different kind of sadness and you help them to heal with your kindness. Same goes to your witty husband, Menno Menist. Thank you for welcoming me to your family. The hug that we shared in the kitchen after the news of this book offer came is something that I will always remember. Thanks also to Olga, Roche and Nina for the family love, and Sammy (rest in peace) for not biting me all the time.

A fun fact about the recipes in this book, is that they were all created and tested in London, The Hague, Delft, Breda and Rotterdam. I simply hate food waste hence and all the food was given away to my Personal Assistant, Sandy Ni in The Hague to share with her neighbours and also her daughter, Avery. They both thought the jackfruit in the biryani recipe was chicken and loved it all the same! We also made sure to donate food to people affected by the pandemic after losing their incomes in Rottterdam.

Sandy, thank you for your amazing support throughout the years. For all the walks in the park and along Scheveningen beach with Avery when I was at my lowest. Having a positive person like you and Avery around helps to boost back my confidence.

Eric van Duin in Delft, thank you for the friendship. You taught me the best way to eat the shared duck dish with rice in a bowl.

Thank you to all my peers in the industry who I cooked with online during the pandemic, Francis Bakt, Nora French, Brian Mellor, Nick Wong, Graeme Fox and Alan Rosenthal, and special thank to Tim Browne from University of Breda for the ongoing support.

Another fun fact about the recipes, quite a few actually had been enjoyed and approved by the ginger cat, Rufus in London who patiently waited for my online cooking demos to finish for him to enjoy the dishes I cooked. Thank you Eric Lam for being the best friend that anyone could ever have asked for and always taking great photos of good memories. Paul, I have known you for years and you could not keep up with my travels back and forth between London and Amsterdam. Thank you for always welcoming my London stays.

A genuine and warm friendship I get from Maureen Duke is something that I will always treasure. Thank you for allowing me to include your delicious recipes. Thank you also to Richard and Trisha Duke for the ongoing friendship and support.

To my restaurant family, Kuala Lumpur Restaurant & Bar in Leeds. I believe that you have to be with the right people, at the right time and location for amazing things to happen. My one month stay training the kitchen team at the restaurant ended up being permanent, something that I never imagined would happen and was one of many great decisions made during the pandemic. Thank you Hirman and Bart for this great opportunity and same to the kitchen and front of house teams, Irwan, Kat, Dil, Chloe, Jake, Barbie, Dominic, Jack, Ruby, Millie, Raphael, Rohan and Eliot. Same to Suzy, Dinny and John for the catering team.

This book would not had happened without the lovely sponsors that kindly offered their products. A massive thank you to Denby Pottery for the beautiful bowls. I am a big fan and always carry my favourite Denby bowl everywhere I move. Same goes to Dok Cookware in The Hague, Domenico Trinchillo in particular for loaning me the beautiful bowls transporting with Eurostar to London from Rotterdam for the photoshoot.

Thanks also to Janice Gabriel for introducing me to Pro Tempeh, London based and independent tempeh producer. Definitely the best tempeh I ever tasted. Thank you Olivier and Amalia for allowing me using your high quality tempeh for the photoshoot. Great thanks to Will Chew of MakTok for the Malaysian sambal.

To all the cookery schools in the UK and Netherlands - The Foodworks, The Cookery School at Braxted Park and Keizer Culinaire, and the previous schools I taught at in the past Leiths School of Food and Wine and Harborne Food School, thank you for allowing me to share my knowledge and passion with your guests.

Finally, to all my social media supporters, I am truly honoured for the ongoing support I keep on getting from around the world. If I had a superpower, it would be to cook for every single one of you to show my thanks for every kind word and like on my social media platform.

Index

A

B

C

D

E

F

G

H

J

K

L

M

N

P

Q

R

T

V

W

Pavilion
An imprint of HarperCollins*Publishers* Ltd
1 London Bridge Street
London SE1 9GF

www.harpercollins.co.uk

HarperCollins*Publishers*
1st Floor, Watermarque Building
Ringsend Road Dublin 4
Ireland

10 9 8 7 6 5 4 3 2 1

First published in Great Britain by HQ,
an imprint of HarperCollins*Publishers* Ltd 2022

Norman Musa asserts the moral right to be identified as the author of this work. A catalogue record for this book is available from the British Library.

ISBN 978-1-91-168232-5

This book is produced from independently certified FSC™ paperto ensure responsible forest management.

For more information visit:
www.harpercollins.co.uk/green

Reproduction by Rival Colour Ltd, UK
Printed and bound in China

Commissioning Editor: Cara Armstrong
Copyeditor: Stephanie Evans
Proofreader: Anne Sheasby
Indexer: Isabel McLean
Design Manager: Laura Russell
Photography: Luke J Albert
Food Styling: Nicole Herft and Holly Cochrane
Prop styling: Nicoel Herft
Art Direction & Design: Evi-O.studio | Susan Le
Design Assistants: Evi-O.studio | Katherine Zhang
& Wilson Leung

WHEN USING KITCHEN APPLIANCES PLEASE ALWAYS FOLLOW THE MANUFACTURER'S INSTRUCTIONS